The Church, A Reluctant Warrior?

Spiritual Warfare – The Church as an Army

Mark Dunman

Freedom
Publishing

ISBN: 978-1-908154-68-2

Freedom Publishing
49 Kingmere, South Terrace,
Littlehampton, BN17 5LD, United Kingdom
www.freedompublishing.net

British Library Cataloguing in Publication Data. A catalogue record for this book is available from the British Library.

Unless otherwise stated, all scripture quotations are taken from The Holy Bible, English Standard Version (ESV) is adapted from the Revised Standard Version of the Bible, copyright Division of Christian Education of the National Council of the Churches of Christ in the U.S.A. All rights reserved.

KJV are taken from The Authorized (King James) Version of the Bible ('the KJV'), the rights in which are vested in the Crown in the United Kingdom, is reproduced here by permission of the Crown's patentee, Cambridge University Press.

NIV are taken from Holy Bible, New International Version® Anglicized, NIV® Copyright © 1979, 1984, 2011 by Biblica, Inc.® Used by permission. All rights reserved worldwide.

Formatted by Freedom Publishing
Cover by Esther Kotecha, EKDesign
Printed in the United Kingdom

CONTENTS

Acknowledgements

Mark has provided us with a clear, thorough and biblical appraisal of the spiritual battle that affects the lives of every follower of Jesus, whether we choose to acknowledge that battle or not. Mark is encouraging the Church to recognise and participate in its true destiny of being active against the spiritual ruler of this world. He explains that such participation needs to be from a place of unity, discipline, intercession and complete obedience to the leading of Jesus, the Commander of the Lord's army. I have been genuinely inspired by the bold but gracious call to arms that Mark has presented through the pages of this book.

David Cross
(Executive member of Ellel Ministries International)

The Lord uses many analogies in the Word to help us better understand the Body of Christ. The picture of the Church as an army has not been explored as deeply as it should, and as a result the believers have not been militant or intentional enough to take ground for the Kingdom. The results are heartbreaking in society. Mark Dunman has produced a writing that should be a 'must' for every group that takes seriously the authority we have been given to deal with the enemy. Let's take our place in the ranks of the Soldiers of the King!

Brenda Taylor of Dovetail Shalom Ministries

A much-needed wake-up call for the Church! Mark Dunman challenges the Church to question whether it is doing enough to engage in the spiritual battle raging on earth today. He suggests that the Church could do so much more to muster its resources and members to fight this battle. He gives a clear, concise overview of the spiritual battle, and then provides Biblical guidelines for the Church to prepare and participate in spiritual warfare to reap the fruits of victory. He argues that the most powerful expression of spiritual warfare will come **when the Church unites and co-ordinates its activities in towns and cities across the world – when it truly becomes the army of God.** The Church needs to rise up in the power that Christ has given us through His death on the cross. This is a timely book as we face the battle of the ages that will continue until our King returns to reign on earth.

Tony & Kathy Stewart
(The Mount Moriah Trust)

The Church – A Reluctant Warrior? is Mark's third book, following his *Has God really finished with Israel?* (2013) and *The Return of Jesus Christ* (2015). Scripturally, believers are given armour with their hands being trained for battle by the Church. Many now question the role of the Church as a warrior force inside society. Mark's new book makes thought-provoking distinctions between a proactive Satan and fallen human nature. The glossary is immensely valuable and the book is well-written. How else can one write these days within the shadow of the End Times!

Jim Penberthy
(Penberthy Consulting)

FOREWORD

Growing up in what would be considered a conservative, fundamental upbringing, my family often heard our pastor preach on spiritual warfare and the dangers that surround followers of Jesus. Brother Ray spoke frequently of hell as the final destination for those who refuse to put their faith and trust in Jesus. We understood that there was a battle being fought in another realm and the adversary was out to seek and destroy Christ's followers, their witness, and their ability to impact the world with the Gospel of Jesus Christ. We were taught not to give up. We were shown in scripture that we were to put on the full armour of God and fight to protect our character, our beliefs, against our fleshly desires, and to surround ourselves united with other believers. We knew that the battleground was and is every unsaved heart across the world. It was instilled in us that one day there will be a judgement, and all will be called to the throne of God to answer for their sins.

Somewhere along the way, many of Christ's followers in the West have become soft. The Church has ceased to teach of this warfare that is raging. We have spent too much time pining over the love of God and his grace. God's love and grace is real! It is abundant and available to us all, but we cannot look the other way while Satan is attacking. The modern-day Church knows Christ will win the war, but in the meantime we have become complacent and thus willing to lose battle after battle. Soul after soul will be lost. Marriage after marriage will disintegrate. We are willing to neglect our influence in the world because we refuse to engage.

Thankfully Mark Dunman is calling the Church to respond in a way that represents her role in the battle. He is calling her to recognise the battle that is all around; being fought on Satan's turf and by his rules. Through Mark's research and writing he is equipping every man, woman, and child with the tools necessary to engage Satan's antics, recognise his ploys, and to defeat his army. Mark does this by masterfully educating the reader through scripture and by defining the arsenal of tools available to us in the fight.

The frontline troops, as Mark Dunman calls them, are Christ's followers who have been charged with interceding on behalf of mankind through prayer. The Church should lead the way in this effort. The Church should teach and equip their people to fight this battle through prayer. The greatest weapon the Church has in her possession to fight against Satan and his legions of demons is praying to God. Praying protection over believers, for the diminishment of sin, and a harvest of souls. Mark encourages the reader to evaluate their prayer life and challenges them to be strategic in engaging in the warfare that is present in our world. The Church cannot fight the battle by sitting in the basecamp. We must take our prayers to the battlefield and intercede for those who are hurting, for those who are searching, and for those who are lost.

Mark Dunman writes: "The Church is used to dislodge this satanic occupying force and to set the captives free. It is a brilliant strategy because it uses the captives already freed, to fight on behalf of those still waiting to be set free." That is the purpose of engaging in the battle. The objective is to extend the kingdom of God by bringing souls to the saving grace of Jesus.

May God richly bless you as you read this incredible reminder of our responsibility to fight the good fight, to engage in the battle with the hopes of seeing the lost find Jesus.

Brian McFadden
Compassion Pastor
Rush Creek Church – Arlington, Texas USA

PREFACE

I have written two scripture-based books, *The Return of Jesus Christ* (2015) and a now expanded and updated edition of *Has God really finished with Israel?* (2022). I wrote the first book when I realised that the subject of Jesus Christ's return to earth seemed to have dropped out of sight in the Church. Few churches appeared to be preaching the subject, unlike the time when I first became a Christian in the charismatic movement nearly fifty years ago. The second book originated with a God-given passion to see his purposes for Israel fulfilled. Both books have been well received as a faithful exposition of scripture.

I had no plans to write a third book. I knew that I had to have a prompt from God with both a subject and a desire to write. However, during a stay in Israel in 2018, my wife and I entertained an Israeli friend and her Finnish visitor to a meal which was followed by a time of prayer. This Finnish lady began to pray for me, and I then realised it was turning into prophecy. Essentially her message was that I would continue to write. As the foundations of the Church continued to collapse through removal of essential spiritual truths, I would help to restore these truths by exposition of the scriptures.

This gave me the needed prompt and the subject was to hand, as the desire to expose the activities of Satan and his kingdom of darkness and see an effective response from the Church had long burned in my heart.

Sometime after this meeting, a long-forgotten dream came to mind that seemed to reinforce this message. In September 1974, about nine months after becoming a Christian, I had a very vivid dream (which I wrote down) that the Lord was calling me to the Ministry of Defence. My opinion was sought by a senior official about someone who was making dangerous explosives which did not give the usual signs accompanying an explosion. The explosions occurred, but people were not aware of them. This was both a clever and also a dangerous feat and I immediately felt in the dream that this was the work of the devil. I woke feeling both honoured and uncomfortable about such a calling so early in my Christian life. I need not have worried: the Lord made me wait nearly forty years before I put pen to paper with my first book!

I am wise enough to know that my authority to write should not be accepted on the evidence of these two events alone. The first part of this book is about Satan's activities, while the second is about how I think (based on my understanding of scripture) the Church should respond to Satan's activities.

There should be no difficulty with the first part. It is all there in scripture. Much of it may be new to many believers since they have not been taught or read what scripture says about the kingdom of darkness. The sad fact is that, for many Christians, Satan is indeed operating with hidden explosives; social attitudes change and the world and much of Christendom is completely unaware of their source. Where Christians do know about the activities of the devil, they often have no idea of the extent of his activities or how to respond to them. Some Christians go to the other extreme and give him too much attention, but without much to show for it.

I firmly believe this is a Church-wide issue and that God is calling the Church to understand the devil's activities and to take up arms against him, but in a disciplined and organised way; in short, the Church is to be an army and one which engages in spiritual warfare.

I realise that some readers will hesitate at the idea of the Church as an army. They will ask: where in the New Testament does scripture describe the Church as an army? I would simply ask them to assess the evidence I bring to bear on this subject. At the very least, the reader should become aware that we can do something about the activities of Satan in our own lives, even if they remain sceptical that the Church at large should engage in spiritual warfare and function as an army.

Since I first put pen to paper, the coronavirus pandemic has come upon us, with all its grief and upheaval. This has led me to include a chapter on the underground church. The coronavirus has made many Christians consider that we may be entering the last days before Christ's return to earth. This raises the distinct possibility that the Church, even in western countries, may need to operate as an underground church. I recognise that in many parts of the world Christians are severely persecuted, and in several countries the Church has already gone underground. Such churches have far more knowledge and experience than I could possibly bring to the subject.

For dates I have used the more traditional BC and AD (Before Christ and Anno Domini) rather than the modern BCE and CE (Before Common Era and Common Era) which are designed to avoid referring to Christ as Lord! There is a glossary which defines theological and other terms used in the book.

I am very grateful to Pastor Brian McFadden for agreeing to take time out of a busy schedule to write the Foreword to this book. My thanks too, to the people who have taken the trouble to read the manuscript and write a short endorsement. My thesis is an unusual one and not every leader would be willing to write a Foreword or endorse the book. I much appreciate their willingness to do this.

I am grateful to Jim Penberthy for his help and enthusiasm to see this book published; and likewise to my prayer group Watchmen for Israel for praying for and encouraging me in this endeavour. My thanks also go to my publisher David Powell and his team for their professional help and encouragement in this third venture. I should also like to thank my friends Tim and Sandy for suggesting the title for the book.

Once again, I am especially grateful to my wife Margaret for her down to earth wisdom, encouraging me to stick to a deadline and for typing the manuscript. As with my other books, she has at times challenged me on the grounds that if she does not understand what I have written, there is a good probability that my readers will not! I hope that because of these interventions, confusion among my readers will be rather less than it might have been.

One final point: many books have been written about spiritual warfare, but almost all of them approach the subject from the point of view of the individual Christian. They expose the work of our spiritual enemy and how we should deal with him. This book is different: its subject is the Church and how the Church should deal with Satan and his kingdom of evil spirits.

Mark Dunman
November 2023

PART I

SATAN'S DOMINION OVER THE HUMAN RACE

The first section of this book deals with Man's fallen state
and his subjection to the dominion of Satan's kingdom.

CHAPTER ONE
INTRODUCTION

The purpose of this book is to alert the Church[1] to the activities of Satan and what we can do about it. Much of the Church is not aware that we are at war with Satan. They may hold to the verse in Colossians which says that Jesus disarmed the spiritual powers and authorities when he triumphed over them on the Cross (*Colossians 2:15*) and feel there is no need to do more than resist the devil's temptations when they arise. Others may feel that once they have a personal relationship with Christ, they are safe in him (which is true); that talk of the devil is all rather unpleasant and should be left well alone.

So let us start by viewing where we stand in Christ. The verse in Colossians is true. If it were not true, we would have no hope. We should be slaves to Satan forever. Satan has been defeated in the sense that he can no longer hold human beings captive should they choose to accept God's offer of salvation in Christ. God does not force us; we have a choice. However, the book of Ephesians reveals that God not only wants to rescue us, but that he has a purpose for believers who constitute the worldwide Church, once they are saved. Ephesians states:

> *. . . and to bring to light for everyone what is the plan of the mystery hidden for ages in God who created all things, so that through the church the manifold wisdom of God might now be made known to the rulers and authorities in the heavenly places.*
>
> *(Ephesians 3:9-10)*

Satan is described as the prince of the power of the air (*Ephesians 2:1-2*) and these rulers are the fallen angels who administer Satan's kingdom. What God was telling Satan and these rulers is that not only would he open the way for people to be reconciled to God through Christ's death on the Cross, but that his redeemed people, the Church, would have a part to play in extending this salvation to other people. They would help to set them free from Satan's grip and thus help to expand the kingdom of God on earth.

Much of the Church (particularly in the West) has barely glimpsed this role for a glorious church. They may understand the need to pray and to share their faith and invite other people to join them in God's kingdom. The call to evangelism is clearly given at the end of both Matthew's and Mark's gospels, but few Christians understand the extent of the spiritual battle involved.

Satan is an invisible foe, and he has made good use of this to hide his activities. He seeks to prevent Christians understanding their inheritance in Christ. Christians who jog along, happy in their faith but not feeling any need to extend the kingdom of God, are left alone, but Christians who start to do effective things for the kingdom of God can soon feel the displeasure and opposition of Satan's kingdom. For too long he has run rings around individual Christians, but more seriously he has done the same to the Church and its leadership. The history of the Catholic and Protestant churches over the last two thousand years has revealed how effective Satan's activities have been. Individual Christians have been on the defensive and the Church has followed blind alleys.

Many Christians believe (and I am one of them) that we are now in the last days before Christ's Second Advent or return to earth. The Bible has much to say about this.[2] I believe that, as we enter this last phase of church activity, God wants the Church to change. He wants the Church to show its mettle and to use the spiritual equipment he has given it to engage in spiritual warfare. Why does he want this?

Building the Kingdom of God

The purpose of this warfare is not to vanquish Satan from the earth. The Bible is quite clear that this is not going to happen until Christ returns, when Christ himself will lock Satan and his fallen angels up for a thousand years. Before Christ returns, Satan will not only continue to trouble the earth but will be given permission to manifest his evil in the person of the Antichrist. This will not be a comfortable time for Christians, but as the darkness increases the light from the Church will brighten and shine in this darkness.

The purpose of the warfare is to extend the kingdom of God on earth by bringing people to salvation under the Lord's direction *(Psalm 127:1)*. It is not about extending the kingdom of God to governments so that the world becomes a better place, ready to receive Christ. When Jesus comes, the world will be a very dark and chaotic place and he will come to sort it out. I believe Satan will be allowed his day to reveal the utter bankruptcy of his rebellion against God. Extending the kingdom is a heart work as God wants souls who will spend eternity with him.

There is a movement in the Church which believes that the Church's role is not only to win souls for Christ, but also to change government and thus make the world ready to receive Jesus when he returns to earth. It is called '**Dominionism**' and is an expression of the **Postmillenial** view of Christ's second advent. It is a deception, and I will say more about this at the close of this introduction.

In contrast, the Bible makes it clear that the world is going to become a very dark place spiritually. Righteous government is not going to be introduced by the Church; it is going to be done by Jesus when he returns.

As this darkness increases, the Church is called to manifest God's glory by preaching the gospel and helping the Holy Spirit to bring many people to salvation. This has already happened in many parts of the world and the twentieth century saw thousands of people respond to the Gospel through the preaching of great evangelists such as Billy Graham. However, it was also the century of the most destructive wars and upheavals the world has ever seen. It ushered in the nuclear age with its power to destroy humanity. There are millions of Christians worldwide, but this has not brought better government. In his discourse on the Mount of Olives, Jesus told his disciples:

> *For then there will be great tribulation, such as has not been from the beginning of the world until now, no, and never will be. And if those days had not been cut short, no human being would be saved. But for the sake of the elect those days will be cut short.*
>
> *(Matthew 24:21-22)*

This and many other passages suggest a time of enormous destruction of which nuclear war could be a part.

Two themes

There are two great themes which dominate the Bible. The first is the spiritual struggle going on between God's kingdom of light and Satan's kingdom of darkness. The second, much better-known theme is that of the salvation of the human race from sin through the atoning death of Jesus on the Cross.

Many churches and Christians pay scant attention to the first theme while devoting all their attention to the second. This second theme of salvation is of vital importance to every human being, whether they know it or not, and so it is not surprising that the Church has been preoccupied with it.

God is not willing that any should perish, but that all should come to repentance.

(2 Peter 3:9 KJV)

This preoccupation has led the Church to neglect the more fundamental and ancient problem of Satan's spiritual rebellion and the ensuing spiritual conflict between good and evil. If Adam and the human race had not sinned, then salvation would not have been necessary since God's new creation would have been living in harmony with God as he intended. However, the conflict between God and Satan would still have existed and it would still have had to be resolved. God had given Adam and Eve freewill, but in the absence of Satan's temptation in the Garden of Eden it is quite possible that the human race would have remained sinless. The fact that Satan successfully tempted Adam and Eve ushered in the second great theme of the Bible: the need for salvation.

As this book proceeds, I shall elaborate on these two themes. First, however, I wish to state some of the consequences that have arisen from the preoccupation with human salvation, to the detriment of understanding the conflict between good and evil. It is my contention that the major errors in modern Church practice and theology, arise from the failure to understand the significance of Satan's kingdom.

1. The timescale of history

A fundamental error is the failure to understand the timescale involved. For many Christians, young earth creationism has ruled out the possibility that Satan was operating long before the creation of man. There is a whole history from the fall of the cherub Lucifer (Star of the Morning) to his present role as Satan (adversary) in charge of a kingdom of evil. Admittedly the Bible only gives us glimpses of his former existence, but it is enough to establish the existence and operation of his kingdom.

An old earth is essential for accommodating this view of Satan and there is evidence both from the Bible and from science that the earth is indeed very old. Understanding that Satan is an old adversary of God helps us to take the measure of his kingdom and his activities. To believe that he was created in the first week of creation as described at the beginning of Genesis, creates too many contradictions.

However, whether one thinks that Satan was around long before the creation of Adam or that he first sinned in the week of creation, it does not alter the fact of Satan's existence on earth and its evil consequences for the human race. Nor does it impact the measures ordained by God to deal with him. **We can all unite on this, irrespective of our view of the age of the earth.**[3]

2. A limited view of Satan's activities

Many Christians have a very limited view of the devil, his power and his kingdom. As God's adversary and as an invisible spirit, Satan has done a very good job at minimising his presence and carrying on his malevolent activities unbeknown to the human race. For many Christians the principal task of the devil is to tempt them to sin, as he did with Adam and Eve. He is an irritant to the Christian who has come to faith in Christ: apart from resisting his temptations, the devil is to be left well alone.[4] Many do not realise that he has a whole kingdom at his command to deflect the human race from God's revelation through his Son Jesus Christ, and to wreak havoc upon the world.

3. The moral failure of the Church

In Western society this ignorance about the devil has led the Church into moral ambivalence about God's Word. In many churches the Bible is not taken as the Word of God, which is to be followed and obeyed, but rather as a guide to living. Once a person has come to faith in Christ, they can then choose a lifestyle to suit their inclinations and play down biblical passages which might stand in opposition to this lifestyle.

Thus we find parts of the Western Church not only condoning certain lifestyles, but encouraging them. Rather than give a lead itself, much of the Western Church has joined Society's adoption of same-sex marriage, transgender rights, diminution of parental rights as being less important than those of the child and even the right to abortion. These issues are paraded under the banner of human rights, but all of them are contrary to the Word of God.

4. The Church and other faiths

There is also confusion in the Church about the place of other faiths or beliefs. Some Church leaders in the West seek to make an equivalence between Christianity and different faiths along the lines that "all faiths lead to the same God". This dangerous belief is demonstrably untrue in the Bible. The essence of the Christian faith is that God reaches down to mankind with his solution of salvation through Jesus Christ. Man cannot solve the problem of his sinful nature by trying to reach up to God through good works or a better lifestyle. Only God can cleanse us from sin and heal our sinful nature as the following verses demonstrate:

I am the way, and the truth, and the life. No one comes to the Father except through me.

(Jesus speaking in John 14:6)

And there is salvation in no one else, for there is no other name under heaven given among men by which we must be saved.

(The apostle Peter talking about Jesus in Acts 4:12)

5. The significance of Israel

This failure to recognise the significance of the devil has also helped to undermine the significance of Israel to the theme of salvation in the Bible.

Once the human race had sinned, God set in motion a plan for his eternal Son, Jesus Christ, to be born as a human baby and to grow up as a man; in fact to be God-Man. The purpose of this plan was to enable God to die on the Cross and to pay the penalty for our sins. God chose to create a race, the Jewish people, from whom this Saviour would arise. Although Jesus is the Saviour of the world, he was born a Jew and, as the resurrected Christ in heaven, is still a Jew. The Bible makes clear that this race is special to God, even though salvation is extended to the whole human race.[5]

There was a further purpose in creating the Jewish race. These were God's people, and they were supposed to show how a people related to God should live and behave. At Mount Sinai, God gave the Jewish people the Ten Commandments (the moral law) and a set of rules, equivalent to a constitution, for how they should live as a nation. This was to be in contrast with how the surrounding pagan nations lived and behaved.

Satan has succeeded in playing down the significance of the Jewish people, so that much of the Church believes in replacement theology. This is the view that God has finished with the Jewish people as a race and that the Church has taken the place of Israel in God's purposes. Not only has this led to the Church being anti-Semitic over the centuries; it has also led to a failure to understand the unfolding of history.

At several points in history the devil has sought to destroy the Jewish people. In the first instance this was to prevent the First Advent of the Messiah, as the Lamb of God who would take away the sin of the world (*John 1:29*). In the most recent instance this was to prevent his return as the reigning Messiah, an event still in the future. The devil's last attempt manifested itself as the horrific Holocaust of the Jewish people in World War II. Today it manifests itself as an ever-present attempt to destroy the modern nation of Israel.

6. An understanding of the End-times

The downplaying of the spiritual kingdom of darkness has led to several deceptive views of the end-times when Christ returns to earth. Given that many Christians believe – with good reason – that we are now in those end-times, it is very important that we discern what is happening as the return of Christ approaches. One of the deceptions, incidentally, is that Christ is not going to return physically to earth – that his return will be spiritual in nature.

7. Theological error in the Church

Finally, Satan does not confine his activities to deceiving the Church on God's moral laws. He also attempts to deceive the Church on theological matters, matters relating to the structure and role of the Church as it awaits Christ's return. There are plenty of warnings about this in the New Testament. (*Acts 20:29-31; 1 Timothy 4:1; 2 Peter 2:1-2; Jude 4*). This is a particular problem for the evangelical/charismatic part of the Church; those who actually believe in and have a personal faith in Jesus Christ as their Saviour. I will touch on one issue shortly.

The Structure of the Book

Part I of the book starts with a reminder of the person of God – he is holy and awesome and however much we enjoy our salvation and intimacy with God we should never forget this. The next chapter explains the meaning of salvation in Jesus Christ. **The primary task of the Church on earth is to win souls for Christ**, so they escape Satan's kingdom and are saved to spend eternity with God. The rest of Part I deals with Satan's kingdom and all the nefarious activities he directs. The world remains largely unaware of this and so, regrettably, does much of the Church.

Part II deals with how God wants us, and has equipped us, to tackle Satan and his kingdom of darkness. I use the analogy **that the Church is like an army equipped with spiritual weapons of warfare** and furthermore that it needs to act like an army and to use these weapons to be really effective in winning souls for Christ.

Dominionism and the New Apostolic Reformation (NAR)

I know that writing about the Church as an army may alarm some evangelical and charismatic Christians. Part of the Body of Christ is very concerned about excesses going on in parts of the Church, particularly in relation to a broad movement known as the **New Apostolic Reformation** (NAR). Those concerned in the Church believe, and I think that in some cases they are right to believe, that parts of the charismatic movement have been deceived by Satan. Charismatic manifestations of the Holy Spirit can sometimes be a mixture of the Holy Spirit, the flesh and even the demonic. However, we should not throw out the baby with the bath water. Many believers have come to a faith in Jesus through these ministries. Where they have gone astray, we need to pray and direct them back to sound scripture.

I mention this now, because some of the New Apostolic Reformation have emphasised spiritual warfare in their attempts to take the world for Christ. This has given the subject a bad name in some Christian circles, but it should not have done so. Spiritual warfare is a valid and **neglected** part of Church life. Mainstream charismatics may be wary of this subject, but my approach is very different from that of the NAR for the following reasons:

1. I do my very best to adhere to scripture

2. I do not subscribe to **Dominionism**, the theology that the Church will take Governments for Christ and thus prepare the earth for his return. The object of spiritual warfare is two-fold; first and pre-eminently, it is to win souls for Christ and thus expand the kingdom of God in men's hearts. Secondly, it is to set captives free from satanic oppression once they have come into the kingdom. I acknowledge that Satan is very territorial himself and consequently it may be necessary to dislodge him from territory to release the captives.

3. I do want to see the Church wage spiritual warfare, and will discuss how I think this can happen, but it should always be done under the direction of Christ himself through the power of the Holy Spirit. Some leaders in the NAR are taking authority to themselves, arguing that this is what scripture tells them to do, but Jesus made it clear that he would be in charge (*Matthew 28:18-20; Mark 16:19-20; Jesus' word to the Seven Churches in Revelation 2 and 3*).

4. I believe that to remain in a safe place we need always to remember the majesty, holiness and awesomeness of God. We need to be in that secret place with God and to be open to correction by him and by fellow believers.

5. Finally, I think that we need to stick resolutely to the Word of God and its moral imperatives. The Word of God is clear that there is no new revelation to be added to scripture, only revelation about how and when to apply it to our circumstances.

The Church as an army

I intend to demonstrate that the Church has indeed been a reluctant warrior. In fact, it is worse than this. In many parts of the twenty-first century Church, spiritual warfare is an aspect of church life that has often been abandoned altogether. The principal purpose of this book is to demonstrate that this need not be so. There are individual churches and groups of believers all over the world who are prepared to stand up to Satan and are actually doing so, but the Church at large is woefully ignorant about this subject.

Many Christians do not even understand that they have a spiritual enemy. I believe this means we have to look again at what the Lord requires from his Church, particularly as we approach the end-times before Christ's return. We need to clearly define our mission: **our mission is to win souls for Christ and to save them from hell**. To do this effectively I believe we need to confront Satan and his forces, who blind the spiritual eyes of non-believers and trap them in false beliefs and other bondages. To do this effectively I think the Church needs to function as an army. I realise some churches will want to avoid this idea, but others may welcome it.

This idea of the Church as an army will be new to many readers. I argue the case for this from scripture, but each reader must decide whether this is a valid application of scripture. I refer to Derek Prince, one of the twentieth century's great Bible teachers, who wrote a book *War in Heaven*, and who had a vision of the New Testament end-time Church as a great army. I think I can substantiate this view from scripture, but once again each reader must assess whether I have done this satisfactorily.

Historically the Church does not seem to have taken on board its role as an army[6]. A notable exception has been the Salvation Army. These Christians adopted a uniform and ranks in pursuit of William Booth's vision to bring the gospel, along with social improvement, to the poor in the East End of London in the late nineteenth and early twentieth centuries. The Salvation Army continues to this day, now operating in 131 countries. The impact of William Booth and his army was immense, leading to increased social awareness and legislation against practices such as people trafficking and child prostitution.

However, I do not think the Salvation Army envisaged warfare in the way proposed in this book. They were essentially evangelists with a social mission to the poor and disenfranchised in society. They would certainly have recognised the devil as the force behind the squalor suffered by the poor and would have resisted his influence through prayer, evangelism, and good works.

Whatever readers think about the idea of the Church as an army, I am convinced that the Church in general needs to become wiser about the enemy's activities and to rebut them. Where there is teaching about Satan, it tends to be about taking defensive action – how Christians can protect themselves. Surely if the Church can take defensive action, it is only one step away from saying: "Let's go on the offensive and take the battle to the enemy!" We must also ask why the apostle Paul said, "we wrestle not against flesh and blood, but against principalities and powers" (*Ephesians 6:12 KJV*), if that does not mean active warfare against Satan's kingdom.

My emphasis may be wrong, but it is a passion that has burned in my heart for many years, and I feel it is right to express it.

Conclusion

A proper "dividing of the Word of Truth" (*2 Timothy 4:16*) demonstrates that while salvation is vitally important to every human soul, the conflict between the forces of good and those of evil is being worked out throughout history. History will have a dramatic finale: the defeat of Satan and the triumph of God. Furthermore, God will have a people who have chosen to love and worship him through acceptance of Christ's death on the Cross. Satan and his forces of darkness, and those souls who refuse God's offer of salvation, will be banished from his presence. It is vital for the Church to understand what is going on before it falls into further deception. Later chapters will expand the points listed above.

In Chapter 3, I will present a summary of the theme of salvation so that the reader is clear about this important subject before we go on to consider the theme of conflict between good and evil. All the information is in the Bible, but it must be unearthed and put together – that is how the Lord has chosen to reveal himself to us. I should also explain that where there is supposition in my arguments, I shall make this clear. I am a scientist by training and so correct assessment of the evidence is very important to me.

Finally, there is another very important reason why Christians need to be aware of the activities of the kingdom of darkness. **God is a holy God,** and we are called to be holy as well:

> *For I am the Lord your God. Consecrate yourselves therefore, and be holy, for I am holy.*
> *(God's instructions to the Israelites in Leviticus 11:44)*

The apostle Paul reveals in the New Testament that Jesus is returning for his Church as a spotless bride:

> *That he [Jesus] might present it to himself a glorious Church, not having spot, or wrinkle, or any such thing; but that it should be holy and without blemish.*
> *(Ephesians 5:27)*

As already mentioned, many Christians believe we are now in the last days before Jesus Christ's physical return to earth. By his Holy Spirit he is working to prepare us all for his day of return. In order that we should become this holy, spotless bride, the whole Church needs to be aware of Satan's plans to upset this process. The next chapter will examine the subject of holiness.

NOTES

1. I define what I mean by the Church in Appendix 1.

2. A full account of various views on the Second Advent can be found in my book *The Return of Jesus Christ*, obtainable from Christian bookshops and on Amazon.

3. Young earth creationists do not face up to the problems created by their view. For example, if Satan was created in the first week of creation with all the other angels in heaven, when did he first sin by rebelling against God? Why was he in the Garden of Eden so soon after his creation and fall from grace? It is indisputable that Satan sinned before Adam otherwise he would not have been in a position to tempt Adam and Eve to sin. **However, this debate needs to be left to another book!**

4. In fairness to Christians who come from the developing nations such as Africa and countries in the East, they may be very aware that pagan practices are associated with demonic spirits before they come to faith in Christ.

5. The proviso, of course, is that each human being has to accept this salvation for themselves, before it takes effect in their lives.

6. I am not referring to the Crusades of the early Middle Ages. These soldiers may have been Christian in name but were anything but Christian in behaviour. They did enormous harm to the reputation of the Church in the following centuries.

CHAPTER TWO
GOD IS A HOLY GOD

It is good to remind ourselves of who God is, especially when we start to examine Satan and his kingdom of darkness. The reality is that God could send Satan and his fallen angels immediately to their eternal destiny in hell, but he has chosen not to do this and we will examine why in a later chapter.

The first foundation of our faith which the Church must restore is an appreciation of God's holiness. If we get this right, the other great foundations of the Church will more easily fall into place.

Our God is an awesome God! God is eternal: he has always existed, and he has created the universe and everything we are aware of. He has revealed his characteristics to us in the Bible. Our God is infinite, a concept that we finite beings find difficult to grasp. As an infinite being, God is omniscient (all-seeing), omnipresent (present everywhere) and omnipotent (all powerful). He is sovereign – nothing whatsoever happens without his permission. He is faithful and unchanging – totally reliable. He is good and righteous (just), but he is also merciful. He is a triune God – he is one God, but exists as three distinct persons: Father, Son and Holy Spirit. These three persons are united – they are in complete agreement over everything they do. God radiates the light of his glory, so much so that we could not see his glory in full and survive (*Exodus 33:20*).

God's holiness

However, the attribute more than any other which makes God so awesome is his holiness. As John MacArthur says[1]:

> *When the angels worship in heaven, they do not say "eternal, eternal, eternal", "faithful, faithful, faithful" or wise, wise, wise" . . . . . they say, "holy, holy, holy is the Lord God, the almighty".*
> *(See Revelation 4:8, Isaiah 6:3).*

Holiness describes the moral excellence and perfection of God. He is not touched by anything impure. It means that many of his other attributes follow from this: his righteousness, his sense of justice and so on. God cannot contemplate or tolerate sin. It is absolute anathema to him. This means that he exercises judgement over sin which cannot go unremarked or unpunished. To tolerate or excuse sin would be to compromise God's holiness. His holiness is one hundred per cent or nothing at all!

We are utterly separated from God's holiness by our sin. There is a huge chasm between God and us and there is nothing we ourselves can do to bridge this gaping hole. Our fallen nature is such that we are unable to see the awfulness of our sin in God's eyes, unless the Holy Spirit enlightens us. Many are the testimonies of Christians who have felt utterly bereft when the Holy Spirit has done this. It has led many to decide to keep short accounts with God: confessing sin immediately they become aware of it, or before they take communion.

The wonder is that God has made a way for man to be reconciled and brought into communion with him despite our sinful nature and sinful acts. As we shall see in the next chapter, this is the solution enacted by Jesus' death on the Cross and his subsequent resurrection.

Isaiah – a man undone!

Let us see how one of the Old Testament prophets felt when in a vision he saw the glory of the Lord. Isaiah was ushered into the presence of the Lord and was so shaken by what he saw that he said:

> *Woe is me! For I am lost [ruined]; I am a man of unclean lips, and I dwell in the midst of a people of unclean lips; for my eyes have seen the King, the Lord of hosts!*
>
> *(Isaiah 6:5)*

The marvellous thing was that Isaiah was not left in this wretched state. Scripture continues:

> *Then one of the seraphim flew to me, having in his hand a burning coal that he had taken with tongs from the altar. And*

he touched my mouth and said: "Behold, this has touched your lips; your guilt is taken away, and your sin atoned for."

(Isaiah 6:6-7)

Isaiah was never the same again. He heard the Lord asking: *"Who will talk to this people [Israel]?"* Immediately Isaiah offered to go and became one of the great Old Testament prophets. Like Isaiah, we too have been redeemed, reconciled to God by accepting what Jesus has done for us on the Cross. This means that we too can have fellowship with God and enjoy his presence in worship and prayer.

Remembering who God is

God does indeed want us to have sweet fellowship with him, but his holiness is a reminder that we need to remember who he is. His attitude to us changes when we become believers, but his nature does not. We must never take liberties with Almighty God and one of the most important things we must not do is to take liberties with his Word, the Bible. Today we find many church leaders contradicting the Word of God. The underlying attitude seems to be that if a lifestyle is loving, or does not harm people, then it must be all right with God. After all, the Bible says:

God is love, and whoever abides in love abides in God, and God abides in him.

(1 John 4:16)

However, the following verse goes on to say:

. . . that we may have confidence for the day of judgement.

(1 John 4:17)

We must not take scripture out of context. Rightly dividing the Word of God means taking all scripture together; not choosing the parts we like and dismissing the parts we do not like.

The outworking of God's holiness

To understand the importance of holding scripture in balance, we need to look at some of the examples where God's holiness has not been respected and how God has responded. Most illustrations are found in the Old Testament, but there are some in the New Testament as well.

God's judgement

The first point to make is that God's judgement is spoken about time and again in scripture. There is judgement on Israel, there is judgement on nations and there is judgement on individuals. When it comes to eternity, there are two judgements: the first is the Great White Throne Judgement for all unrepentant sinners (*Revelation 20*) and the second is the Judgement Seat of Christ for believers. The Judgement Seat of Christ is very different from the Great White Throne Judgment: believers will not experience this judgement with its eternal punishment, but their life and work on earth for the kingdom of God will be assessed. Those whose life is seen as gold or silver will receive rewards, while those whose life is seen as straw and stubble will suffer loss. All however will be accepted into heaven (*1 Corinthians 3:12-15*).

As already mentioned, there are many examples of God's judgement in the Old Testament, but I want us to look at some examples where God's holiness was affronted.

The death of Aaron's sons

Aaron and his four sons were chosen by God and were being trained for the priesthood of Israel. God's stipulation as to how these things were to be done was very clear and very precise, and he did not allow for any laxity. In *Leviticus 10*, the writer explains how two of the sons, Nadab and Abihu, put fire in their censers and added incense to the fire. It says:

> *They offered unauthorized fire before the Lord, contrary to his command.*
>
> *(Leviticus 10:1)*

The consequence was that fire came out from the presence of the Lord and burnt them and they died before the Lord. Moses' comment to his shaken brother, Aaron, was:

This is what the Lord spoke of when he said: "Among those who approach me I will show myself holy; in the sight of all the people I will be honoured."

(Leviticus 10:3)

The death of Uzzah

This is the story of what happened when the Philistines, who had captured the Ark of the Covenant, decided to return it to Israel (*2 Samuel 6*). After its capture by the Philistines, God showed his displeasure by afflicting the people of Ashdod with tumours. The people had had enough and sent the Ark back to Israel! It arrived at Abinadab's house in Gibeah (close to Jerusalem) where it remained for twenty years. When King David captured the city, he decided to bring the Ark to Jerusalem and Abinadab's sons, Uzzah and Ahio, were tasked to lead the oxen towing the cart which carried the Ark. At one point the oxen stumbled and the Ark was at risk of falling from the cart. Uzzah put out his hand to hold the Ark in place, but with devastating consequences:

And the anger of the Lord was kindled against Uzzah; and God struck him down there because of his error, and he died there beside the Ark of God.

(2 Samuel 6:7)

One cannot help but feel sympathy for Uzzah, but the fact was that God had decreed that only the Levites and priests could approach the Ark. Knowingly or otherwise Uzzah had stepped beyond God's line of demarcation and suffered the consequences. The reality is that God's holiness must be treated with the utmost respect.

The death of Ananias and Sapphira

We now come to one example of God's judgement in the New Testament. God's holiness was affronted by Ananias and Sapphira lying to the Holy Spirit (in other words to God himself). It is an interesting as well as a salutary story, found in *Acts 5*.

The young church was thriving and being a blessing in Jerusalem. Scripture says that the apostles were testifying with great power and grace was upon them all. New believers were sharing possessions so that no one was in need. People with property were selling houses and land so that the proceeds would bless the whole community.

Ananias and Sapphira sold a piece of property but kept back part of the proceeds. They told the apostles that they were giving the whole proceeds to the community. Immediately the Holy Spirit alerted Peter to what was happening. Peter was in fact given a word of knowledge about the situation and he prophesied judgement, leading to the death of both Ananias and Sapphira. The sin was not the failure to give the whole sum, but to pretend that they had; in short, they had lied. Peter's words are worth reflecting on:

Ananias why has Satan filled your heart to lie to the Holy Spirit and to keep back for yourself part of the proceeds of the land? While it remained unsold, did it not remain your own? And after it was sold, was it not at your disposal? Why is it that you have contrived this deed in your heart? You have not lied to men, but to God.

(Acts 5:3-4)

Not surprisingly the young church was greatly shaken by this experience of God's righteous anger. The scripture says:

And great fear came upon the whole church and upon all who heard these things.

(Acts 5:11)

God's glory manifested in Solomon's temple

After these very salutary illustrations we can relate one story from the Old Testament about God's glory and holiness which was not judgemental. It reflects God's pleasure at being honoured by King Solomon and the Israelites. Nevertheless, as the reader will see, it left some people prostrate!

The occasion was the bringing of the Ark of the Covenant, which had been housed in the Tabernacle from the time of Moses until King Solomon's reign, into the newly built temple. Solomon had spent much time and money creating a temple to be God's dwelling place on earth[2]. This day was a special occasion and God honoured it in a special way, giving it his seal of approval. This is how he did it:

And when the priests came out of the Holy Place, a cloud filled the house of the Lord, so that the priests could not stand to minister because of the cloud, for the glory of the Lord filled the house of the Lord.

(1 Kings 8:10-11)[3]

Conclusion

These stories are a timely reminder that we must respect God's holiness at all times. Today in the Church at large, there is an imbalance. We major on the love of God expressed through what Jesus did for us on the Cross and forget that Jesus himself is also described as a formidable judge!

The apostle, John, who had been so close to Jesus on earth, described in *Revelation 1* how Jesus appeared to him as an awesome figure. So much so, that John fell at his feet as though dead. In response to this Jesus did not soften his demeanour for old times' sake! He said:

Fear not, I am the First and the Last, and the living one. I died, and behold I am alive for evermore, and I have the keys of Death and Hades. Write therefore the things that you have seen . . . .

(Revelation 1:17-19)

Jesus then went on to dictate the messages to the seven churches in Asia Minor (modern-day Turkey). What is fascinating is that these messages show both Jesus' great love for his Church, but also his strictness. His message is very direct and sometimes sharp. The modern-day Church would be wise to learn from these messages (as well as from the whole of scripture) what is required of it. If Jesus condemns the idolatry of the Nicolaitans and the sexual immorality in the church of Pergamon and Thyatira, then we too should shun the corresponding behaviours in today's churches.

Being holy is to be separated to God and thus to be separated from all that which is not holy.

NOTES

1. *Our Awesome God* by *John MacArthur* P.38

2. As an infinite being God is everywhere, but the Bible indicates that he can direct his presence to a particular place at a particular time. There is, if you like, a special presence of God, such as that found in and around the Ark of the Covenant.

3. This reminds us of what happens when the people are ministered to and fall down under the power of the Holy Spirit (sometimes called "slain in the Spirit"). My personal view is that on this occasion in the temple, God's glory was seen visibly as a golden cloud, known as his Shekinah glory.

CHAPTER THREE
THE THEME OF REDEMPTION AND SALVATION

Before we examine the conflict between the kingdom of light (God's kingdom) and the kingdom of darkness (Satan's kingdom), we need to explain the meaning of salvation through Jesus Christ. It is vital that we understand this and decide where we stand in relation to God. For those readers who are already believers you may wish to skip this chapter, but I do recommend that you read the summary of the "Exchange made at the Cross" at the end of the chapter.

As the book proceeds, we shall touch on scientific and other sources of knowledge, but it is essential to understand that the Bible is our principal source of information. The Bible is God's Word to us, the human race. The Old and the New Testaments constitute a seamless whole; we cannot have one without the other. Jesus Christ is the person who links them together. I shall provide a summary on how to approach the Bible in Appendix 3.

Whole books have been written on the theme of salvation and I do not intend to provide a full exegesis in this one. However, we do need to be clear what it means before we proceed with the rest of the book.

Salvation is a very clear change in a person's life, and it is understandable that a person, newly saved, will be pre-occupied with this and how to please God in their daily lives. However, for them to fully understand the implications of the change in their life it will be necessary to go further into the things of God as disclosed in the Bible.[1]

Salvation and what it means

Many people believe that if they live a good life, say their prayers and help other people that they will be accepted by God. The Bible is very clear that this alone is not sufficient to find salvation.

Let us look at what salvation really means to understand why it is so important. The process of salvation involves coming into a personal relationship with the risen Lord Jesus Christ – the resurrected Christ is alive in heaven today and communicates with us by his Holy Spirit.[2]

This personal relationship with Christ is what is meant by being "born again" or becoming an evangelical Christian. There may be many people reading this book who have been faithful churchgoers, perhaps for many years, but who have never understood or made this commitment to Christ. I would especially ask them to follow the teaching of this chapter and see whether they are ready or willing to make this commitment. One can pray the prayer of faith alone or with another Christian present if that is helpful. It is a conversation between you and God. I will include a suitable prayer of faith at the end of this chapter.

The origin of sin

The Bible explains both in Genesis and in the book of Romans that all humanity has been placed under the curse of sin through Adam's disobedience to God. Although his wife Eve was the first to sin, the spiritual inheritance of sin came through Adam; the male head of the family and the father of the human race (*Genesis 3:1-19; Romans 5:12-19*).

This means that every human being is born with a disposition to sin. It is an hereditary stain on our human spirit. I do not profess to understand why the disobedience of our first parents gave us this nature. It appears that, just as physical characteristics are inherited through our physical DNA, so the disposition to sin rests within our spiritual DNA.

It reminds us that we do not choose to be born; ultimately we are God's creation and he puts our spirit within us (*Zechariah 12:1*). However, we have free will and, once born and having passed through early childhood, we can choose what to do and the direction we take in life. The biggest choice we must make is whether to accept God's solution to the problem of sin and receive his salvation. God provides the solution, but he will not force us to accept it – that would be a denial of the free will that God has given us.

There is a temptation to complain about the situation into which we are born, carrying the stain of sin. However, we need to remember that God, in his love for the human race, has himself provided a solution – the death of his eternal Son, Jesus Christ in our place on the Cross at Calvary. We could not ask more of God than this, which is why it is so important for human beings to study and accept this sacrificial gift on their behalf.

God is a righteous and just God

God is a righteous God which means that there is a penalty for sin and we have to pay that penalty. The penalty is both physical death of the body and spiritual death or separation from God after our physical death (*Matthew 10:28*).

The only way that another person could pay this penalty in our place would be if they were sinless. That rules out any other human being standing in our place and saying, "I will pay the penalty for you!" He or she has to pay his or her own penalty.

I [Paul] have already charged that all men, both Jews and Greeks [Gentiles], are under the power of sin.

(Romans 3:9)

Surely there is not a righteous man on earth who does good and never sins.

(Ecclesiastes 7:20)

The extraordinary solution that God the Father envisaged was that he would cause his own eternal Son, himself God, voluntarily to be born as a human being. He would grow up to be a man, suffer human temptations, but never sin. Finally, he would die on the Cross in our place, paying the penalty for our sin. This Son, whom we call Jesus Christ, became God-man.

The Bible implies that God the Father poured out his wrath at human sin onto Christ as he lay dying on the Cross 2000 years ago. This is what is meant by propitiation as an atonement for sin (*1 Corinthians 15:3, 2 Corinthians 5:21*). He placed his wrath on Christ for every sin any human being had committed or would commit in the future, while at the same time removing the very stain of sin inherited from Adam.

39

The horror of this experience for the sinless Son of God was revealed in the agony in the Garden of Gethsemane (*Matthew 26:36-46)* and by Christ's plaintive words on the Cross:

My God, my God why have you forsaken me?
(Matthew 27:46, Mark 15:34)

The passion or crucifixion of Christ is referred to many times in both the Old and New Testaments (for example *Psalm 22; Psalm 88; Isaiah 52:13-53:12).* Suffice it to say that we cannot imagine what this suffering was like. Not only did Christ suffer the wrath of God, but scripture suggests he suffered the taunts of Satan and his army of demons (*Psalm 22:12-16).* His physical death on the Cross, horrible as it must have been, was not the principal cause of suffering – this was spiritual.

The resurrection of Christ

The Bible suggests that Christ's spirit descended into Hades, the realm of the dead, for three days (*Ephesians 4:8-10; 1 Peter 3:19-20).*[3] At the end of that time, God the Father raised Christ's spirit from the dead into a new and glorious body; an event known as the resurrection. It is the resurrected Christ, dwelling in heaven, to whom we relate and who speaks to us through his Spirit, the Holy Spirit. This resurrected Christ **will return** to earth in this new body as the God-man, King of both the Jews and the whole of creation.[4]

The significance of the resurrection

The significance of the resurrection is that Christ not only paid the penalty for our sins, but he defeated death itself. Death does not mean extinction of life. A man's spirit, created by God at his conception, is eternal (*Ecclesiastes 12:7).* Death means that the body experiences physical death and that man's spirit experiences eternal separation from God. This was the consequence of Adam and Eve's original sin.

> *Therefore, just as sin came into the world through one man,*
> *and death through sin, and so death spread to all men because*

all sinned . . . .

(Romans 5:12)

For the law of the spirit of life has set you free in Christ Jesus from the law of sin and death.

(Romans 8:2)

Since therefore the children share in flesh and blood, he [Jesus] *himself likewise partook of the same things, that through death he might destroy the one who has the power of death, that is, the devil . . . .*

(Hebrews 2:14)

Jesus' death and subsequent resurrection put an end to this. Man was now free to be reunited with God and experience eternal life, if he so chose to do this.

The apostle Peter has a wonderful passage on Jesus' resurrection (*Acts 2:22-28*) when he says that God loosed the pangs of death because it was not possible for Christ to be held by death. He quotes from the Psalms (*Psalm 16:8-11*) where it implies that while allowing Christ to go through the suffering of the Cross, it then says:

You will not abandon my soul to Hades or let your Holy one see corruption.

(Acts 2:27)

A further consideration is that God raised Jesus from the dead so that he himself might present his own blood before the Father in heaven (*Hebrews 9:12*). What a wonderful seal of approval by the Father for the atoning work of his son Jesus!

The exchange at the Cross

The exchange at the Cross is a crucial phrase. It means that Christ gave his physical life and suffered God's wrath in our place, so that we could be free to be reconciled to God and experience eternal life with all its blessings. It is no wonder that the New Testament is so full of the unmerited blessings for humanity from this transaction.

However, there are two sides to this exchange: Christ has done his part, but we must do ours. The exchange is not automatic. **Our part in the transaction is very straightforward, but we still have to do it.** We have to acknowledge what Christ has done for us on the Cross. We have to confess to God that we have committed sins and to ask him to forgive us. King Solomon said:

> *There is no one who does not sin.*
>
> *(1 Kings 8:46)*
> *(See also: Romans 3:9; 3:23; 5:12 and Ephesians 2:3)*

We have to ask Jesus to come into our life and take control of it. This last process is very important because the Holy Spirit comes to dwell in us and renew our spirit. This is the origin of the expression to be **born again**. (Read Jesus's conversation with Nicodemus in *John 3:1-15*).

This transformation only happens through the action of the Holy Spirit, **but we are required to want this to happen** and that is because God gave us free will. It is an enormous change in our lives because Christ now wants to take charge of us. We have been purchased through Christ's blood and redeemed for God's kingdom. He now wants to begin the process of recreating us in his image.[5]

A work in progress

From the moment of salvation, as ministers often tell their congregations, "we are a work in progress" while we continue our earthly life. We have an on-going relationship with the Lord Jesus Christ. Salvation (sometimes called justification) is instantaneous, but our sanctification is a process, as we are moulded by God's Word and he uses life's experiences to make us more like Christ.

We still have the option to sin because the New Testament makes clear that our old sinful nature continues to reside alongside our new nature (*Colossians 3:1-16*). I would therefore add one further responsibility we have towards God when we accept his salvation – this is to co-operate with his work of regeneration. We will be tempted by the devil to sin (*Matthew 4:1-11; Hebrews 4:15*) and we are required to resist the temptation. If we fail, as sometimes happens, we then need to confess and repent of this sin. The New Testament says that Christ's blood always avails to cleanse us from sin (*Matthew 26:28; 1 John 1:7*).

A summary of the exchange made at the Cross

We can summarise what Jesus did for us on the cross as follows:

1. He was our **substitute**
2. He **paid the penalty** for the collective sin of the human race. (*He bore the wrath of God against sin and suffered physical death and spiritual separation from God. In doing so he satisfied the **justice** of God but permitted God to **forgive** the sinner*).
3. He **set us free** from the **sinful nature**; what the Bible calls the power of sin.
4. He **set us free** from **spiritual death**.

These four things enabled us to be restored to fellowship with God and thus receive eternal life, BUT in doing this Jesus also achieved two other things:

5. He **redeemed** us from the power of Satan and from death and hell (*Revelation 1:18; Colossians 1:13*).
6. He **defeated** Satan and broke his power over men and women (*Colossians 2:15*).

We shall examine these two further achievements in the ensuing chapters.

The prayer of faith

To close this chapter, I include a simple prayer for salvation for those readers who do not yet know Jesus Christ as their personal Saviour.

If you pray this prayer with sincerity and the desire to follow Christ, then you will become saved. The Holy Spirit will regenerate your spirit. You may find this to be an emotional experience, or you may not feel any different, but the **fact** is that you are now a new person in Christ.

Heavenly Father, I now understand that I have sinned against you. I understand too that you sent Jesus to die on the Cross for my sins and that you raised him from the dead. I am truly sorry for my sins. I repent of them and ask you to forgive me. I now ask Jesus to come into my life and renew my spirit so that I may have eternal life. I ask Jesus to take charge of my life as my Saviour and Lord.

Thank you for my salvation.

Once you have prayed this prayer then I urge you to make contact with a Christian or a church and tell them of your decision. You will have made the decision that determines your eternal destiny, but you will need to grow as a Christian through reading the Bible, being taught from it, and having fellowship with other Christians. This is best achieved by joining a church that teaches the truth from the Bible.

I wish you well in your Christian life!

NOTES

1. It is a good idea to read *Romans, Chapters 1 to 8* and *1 Corinthians Chapters 1 & 2* in order to get an idea of the apostle Paul's perspective on the Cross of Jesus.

2. The Holy Spirit is the third person in the Trinity or Godhead of Father, Son (Jesus) and Holy Spirit. They are three distinct persons within the One God, united in all that they do.

3. Not all theologians agree that these texts mean that Christ's spirit descended into Hades. However, I think the passage in Ephesians does mean this, and that he freed the righteous Old Testament saints from Paradise, that part of Hades where their spirits had been confined until the time of Christ's crucifixion and resurrection.

4. See my book *The Return of Jesus Christ*

5. The word 'purchased' in this context is interesting. The word purchase means to be purchased from someone or somewhere. We have indeed been purchased from Satan's kingdom; a theme we shall explore as the book proceeds.

CHAPTER 4
SATAN'S RELATIONSHIP TO THE HUMAN RACE

When considering the Christian faith and our relationship with God, it is really important to understand that there are two spiritual kingdoms in the spiritual realm, the righteous kingdom of God and the unrighteous or evil kingdom of Satan, the devil.

It is also important to understand that God runs his kingdom according to ordered and legal principles. He vests his authority in angels and people, and he expects them to operate according to his principles.

We see this first in Genesis when God created man in his image and gave him dominion over the earth. This meant that Adam and his descendants would have authority over all the living creatures on earth and over everything that happened there. In exercising this authority they would be accountable to God. Ultimately the authority is God's, as it is over all of his creation, but Adam and his descendants were authorised to act as his representatives on earth.

What went wrong?

In Chapter 5 we will examine Satan's origin and what went wrong in his relationship with God. For the time being it is important to realise that when Adam and Eve disobeyed God in the Garden of Eden, they came out from under his authority and transferred their allegiance to the devil and therefore came under Satan's authority. They may not have understood this at the time, but the Bible is very clear that this is what happened. Thus we can see that sin led to spiritual separation from God and to humanity coming under another being's authority. The consequences of this single act of disobedience by Adam and Eve have been devastating for the human race.

Down the ages the Church has tended to concentrate only on this broken relationship with God and how this has been repaired by Christ's death on the Cross. This preoccupation with our personal salvation has been understandable; Christ has taken the punishment for our sin on the Cross and we have been set free to be born again into a new relationship with God.

What has not been understood by much of the Church in its long history is the consequence of coming under Satan's authority. The reality of this transference of authority to the devil did not become clear at the time of the original sin of Adam and Eve. In Genesis 3 God punishes Adam and Eve and the serpent, but makes it clear that he will continue to have a relationship with the human race, even though it is a broken relationship. At this point in history the transference of this authority to the devil is not clearly stated, but it becomes apparent as history proceeds in the Old Testament and is abundantly plain by the time of Jesus.

Satan's spiritual kingdom

Satan's control over the earthly kingdoms is revealed in a number of scriptures and it is good to take a look at the principal verses.

The significance of the first scripture is often overlooked. Jesus was tempted on three occasions by the devil during his forty days of fasting in the Judean wilderness. In the third temptation Satan took Jesus to a high place where he *"showed him all the kingdoms of the world and their glory"* and then said, *"All these I will give you if you will fall down and worship me." (Matthew 4:8-9).*

Today, we baulk at the effrontery of the devil's words to the eternal Son of God! However, Jesus' reply is very interesting. He did not say to Satan, "These are not your kingdoms to give away, they belong to God." He said instead, *"Be gone, Satan! For it is written: 'you shall worship the Lord your God and him only shall you serve.'" (Matthew 4:10).* Jesus clearly recognised that these human kingdoms were under Satan's control.[1]

Here are some further scriptures which relate both to Satan's spiritual kingdom in the mid heavens[2], and to his control over the earthly kingdoms.

> *He [God] has delivered us from the domain of darkness and transferred us to the kingdom of his beloved Son.*

(Colossians 1:13)

*But you are a chosen race, a royal priesthood, a holy nation, a people for his own possession, that you may proclaim the excellence of him **who called you out of the darkness into his marvellous light.***
(1 Peter 2:9) [emphasis added]

*We know that we are from God, and **the whole earth lies under the power of the evil one.***
(1 John 5:19) [emphasis added]

*In their case **the god of this world** has blinded the minds of the unbelievers, to keep them from seeing the light of the gospel of the glory of Christ, who is the image of God.*
(2 Corinthians 4:3-4) [emphasis added]

*Now is the judgement of this world; now will **the ruler of this world** be cast out.*
(John 12:31) [emphasis added]

*. . . for the **ruler of this world** is coming. He [Satan] has no claim on me [Jesus] . . .*
(John 14:30) [emphasis added]

Jesus clearly calls Satan the ruler of this world. His kingdom is described as one of darkness, while God's kingdom is described as one of light. We frequently come across the terms light and dark in the scriptures to define a spiritual reality.

Additional scriptures reinforce this perception of Satan's hold over the human race.

For we wrestle not against flesh and blood, but against principalities, against powers, against the rulers of the darkness of this world, against spiritual wickedness in high places.
(Ephesians 6:12 KJV)

As we shall discover in more detail later in the book, believers are involved in this spiritual conflict every time they pray or proclaim the Word of God.

Two of these principalities are mentioned in the Old Testament in the book of Daniel. The angel Gabriel tells Daniel that he was delayed in response to Daniel's prayer to God by the Prince of Persia and that he only succeeded in coming to him with the help of the archangel Michael (*Daniel 10:10-14*). It is clear from the context that this prince is a spiritual being, one of the principalities or powers, and that he has authority over the nation of Persia and its human rulers.

Later we learn that the Prince of Persia would be followed by the Prince of Greece (*Daniel 10:20*). This conflict in the heavenlies (the spiritual realm) was enacted on earth when the King of Greece, Alexander the Great, defeated the King of Persia (Darius III) in the Battle of Issus in 333 BC. The Greek Empire superseded the Medo-Persian Empire from this point on.

Satan's kingdom is a kingdom of conflict with principalities and powers wrestling with each other for dominance. This is reflected in what happens on earth, one worldly empire being displaced by another, as in the example above. One really important message for Christians to realise is that while human leaders and kingdoms come and go, the powers behind them do not. They are eternal spiritual beings with territorial responsibilities on earth and they rise and fall according to the conflicts in Satan's dominion of darkness. Today we see that the power behind the Persian Empire is still around and is coming to prominence once again, but in a different guise as the Persian nation (Iran) rises up as a dominant Islamic nation with the declared aim of destroying Israel. We do not see the conflicts taking place in the spiritual realm, but we do see the consequences of these conflicts here on earth.

Very occasionally God lifts the veil hiding spiritual conflicts from human view. A famous example is the vision God gives to Elisha's servant when Israel and Elisha are threatened by the king of Syria and his army. The servant is afraid and dismayed when he sees their city (Dothan) surrounded by Syrian chariots and horses, but Elisha reassures him. He says:

> *Do not be afraid, for those who are with us are more than those who are with them.*
>
> *(2 Kings 6:16)*

He then asks the Lord to open the servant's eyes to the spiritual reality. He is shown a mountain full of horses and chariots of fire surrounding and protecting Elisha. (The full account is given in *2 Kings 6:8-23*).

In a later chapter we shall discuss the influence of Christian prayer and proclamation of God's Word on these conflicts in the spiritual realm. Satan has plans and purposes, but these can be thwarted by God in response to the prayers and intercessions of God's people. Sadly, much of the Church is not aware of the spiritual battle that God has called his saints to undertake.

We can reasonably assume on the basis of what we read in the book of Daniel that the world is divided up into empires and nations, each with a governing satanic spirit. The Church with its praying Christians stand in opposition to these powers, so the extent of their influence will depend on how effective the Church is in any given country. We will learn more on this in a later chapter.

Satan's kingdom: what Christ achieved on the Cross

We saw at the end of the last chapter that Jesus not only purchased our salvation, but that he also defeated Satan and broke his power. We have to take hold of this victory over sin and Satan by coming into a personal relationship with Christ for these benefits to operate. Until individuals take this step of accepting Christ as their Saviour, they are still under the power of Satan. God gives us that responsibility to accept or reject what Christ has done for us on the Cross. It is a shock for people and even Christians to learn that until they are saved, they are captives to Satan's kingdom.

This has the important consequence that Satan still has power over the kingdoms of the earth; he is still in charge. Nevertheless, he loses a captive every time someone gives his or her life to Christ. God can then add this new believer to his army of Christians and calls them to challenge the power of Satan through prayer and preaching the Word of God. In this way more captives take the decision to leave their captivity and be reconciled to God. Even more significantly, these believers are saved to spend eternity with God.

The legal nature of the Exchange made at the Cross

It is very important to understand that God has organised his kingdom, and the way he rules the universe, on a legal basis. The legal constitutions of Western democracies, such as Britain and the United States are said to be based on Judeo-Christian principles. This means that they operate according to the principles expounded in the Bible. The underlying principle is that relationships should be conducted on the basis of mutual respect according to the Ten Commandments. Jesus explains that the principle undergirding the Ten Commandments is that we should love God and love our neighbour as ourselves.

This means that when this mutual respect is not observed through breaking a commandment, that an offence has been committed and that this must be punished. The defendant is said to be guilty of a crime and this must be redressed by suffering a penalty and when possible making amends for this crime.

The exchange made at the Cross was a legal one, as illustrated in the following verse:

> .... by cancelling the record of debt that stood against us **with its legal demands**. This he [Jesus] set aside, nailing it to the Cross. He disarmed the rulers and authorities and put them to open shame, by triumphing over them in it [the Cross].
> *(Colossians 2:14-15)* [emphasis added]

It is true that God in his great mercy and love, wanted to re-establish a relationship with the fallen human race, but he would not undermine his own legal principles to bring this about and rescue us. Satan had deceived Adam and Eve, but by giving into temptation they had ceded their authority to Satan. He now had a right to say that the human race and its kingdoms were his, to do what he liked with.

Man could not get out of this situation; he was truly lost and a slave to Satan's kingdom. We may feel this was a harsh consequence of Adam and Eve's single sin, given that we know what it is like to struggle with temptation and sin (read Paul's struggle in *Romans 7*), but we have to remember that Adam and Eve gave into temptation from a position of purity. They were perfect, as beings created in the image of God and so it should have been easier for them to say no, especially as God had spoken to them in person as to what they could and could not eat.

In Chapter 5 we shall see that Satan too existed in a state of perfection as the anointed cherub, Lucifer. Like Adam and Eve, he too had free will. He became proud which led to his rebellion against God.

The only way that the human race could be extracted from this dire state was for the legal penalty to be paid by a sinless human being. As we saw in the previous chapter, the only sinless being to do this was God himself, present on earth in the form of a man. This is why *Colossians 2:15* says that Satan and his rulers were defeated and disarmed at the Cross. Satan's legal right to hold humanity captive was broken because the sinless Son of God had paid the penalty in our place. The following verses reveal this:

> *Whoever makes a practice of sinning is of the devil, for the devil has been sinning from the beginning. The reason the Son of God appeared was to destroy the works of the devil.*
> *(1 John 3:8)*

> *Now is the judgement of this world; now will the ruler of this world be cast out.*
> *(Jesus talking to the people in John 12:31)*

The cosmic conflict

Therefore, what can we conclude about Satan and his relationship to God? From the time of Lucifer's fall from grace to becoming God's adversary, Satan, there has been a cosmic conflict between God's kingdom of light and Satan's kingdom of darkness. At this stage in history, one that has extended for the last 6000 years, the human race has been at the centre of this conflict. I wonder how many Christians are fully or even partially aware of his?

In Chapter 5 we shall examine Satan's origins and his fall from grace. This has led me to the conclusion that the most likely explanation of events is that Satan was in charge of an earlier creation which was destroyed when he sinned and rebelled against God. We do not know for how long this creation lasted, but it appears that God started again, this time with the creation of man on a restored earth a few thousand years ago. This is why I think the world and the universe are ancient. However, this is a controversial issue among Christians with different views on the age of the earth and I do not propose to debate the issue in this book. As I said in Chapter 1, Satan is a present reality and it is enough for believers to come to terms with this and to learn how to tackle our spiritual enemy, rather than to be side tracked into a debate about the age of the earth.

When God came to create man, he did something unique which he does not appear to have done with other created beings.[3] In *Genesis 1:26* God said: *"Let us make man in our own image, after our likeness."*[4]

We will examine at a later point why Satan (as a serpent) came to be in the Garden of Eden, and why he had permission to tempt Adam and Eve. The fact that man was created in the image of God goes a long way to explain Satan's enmity towards the human race. Given his own rejection by God, the incentive to derail God's programme in relation to a new race, must have been enormous.

What a success story for Satan, that he and his kingdom of fallen spirits captured a race of beings made in the image of God. The Christian teacher, Derek Prince, put it very succinctly when he said: "Satan cannot get at God directly, but he can get at the image of God, every time he causes a man or woman to stagger down the street drunk!"

God's plan of salvation

God, however, had other plans for this race made in his image. We do not know whether God offered salvation to Satan and his fallen angels and demons, but we do know right from the time of the Fall in the Garden of Eden that God would bring in a plan to redeem this new race. He did not reveal it at the time, but the seeds of his solution were expressed in his words to the serpent:

> *I will put enmity between you and the woman, and between your offspring and her offspring; he shall bruise your head, and you shall bruise his heel.*
>
> *(Genesis 3:15)*

Theologians generally believe this was the first reference to a coming Saviour.

Conclusion

What we see today, and what has been happening throughout human history, is the outworking of this cosmic conflict between God and Satan, and mankind is right at the centre of it! Satan was defeated at the Cross, but he still seeks to thwart the plans of God, pollute the earth with sin and take as many people as possible with him into hell, his final destiny. For Christians waiting to see God save as many people as possible, the stakes could not be higher!

NOTES

1. It is worth noting that as Jesus quotes from the Old Testament he is also highlighting the authority of the written Word of God.

2. I define terms such as mid-heaven and heavenly places in the Glossary.

3. We cannot be sure about this, but great emphasis is put on this aspect of man in *Genesis 1:26-27*.

4. It is generally believed that the plural "us" refers to the Godhead: Father, Son and Holy Spirit.

CHAPTER 5
SATAN: HIS KINGDOM OF FALLEN ANGELS AND DEMONS

I mentioned earlier that the Bible does not devote a lot of space to Satan's origins. However, there are two principal passages in the Old Testament which clearly describe who he was and who he became. These are *Isaiah 14:12 onwards* and *Ezekiel 28:11-19*.

It is important to understand that both chapters commence by describing an earthly king. In Isaiah it is the King of Babylon, while in Ezekiel it is the Prince of Tyre. However, it becomes apparent that the passage moves in both instances to describe a celestial being. At a certain point in both passages the prophet is no longer talking about an earthly king. (In Ezekiel the change is marked by a reference to the King of Tyre rather than the prince). This is an example of what Bible exegesis calls "double reference" – a technique we see several times in the Bible.

The Ezekiel passage describes Satan's creation and existence before his fall, followed by his sin in rebelling against God, while the Isaiah passage deals only with his fall. As these passages are unfamiliar to many Christians, I will quote them in full before analysing what they say. (I suggest the reader reads the whole of each chapter to gain the context of the passages about Satan).

The Ezekiel passage (from *Ezekiel 28:11-19*):

[11] Moreover, the word of the LORD came to me:
[12]Son of man, raise a lamentation over the king of Tyre, and say to him, Thus says the Lord GOD: "You were the signet of perfection, full of wisdom and perfect in beauty:
[13]You were in Eden, the garden of God; every precious stone was your covering, sardius, topaz, and diamond, beryl, onyx, and jasper, sapphire, emerald and carbuncle; and crafted in gold were your settings and your engravings. On the day that

you were created they were prepared.

[14]You were an anointed guardian cherub. I placed you; you were on the holy mountain of God; in the midst of the stones of fire you walked.

[15]You were blameless in your ways from the day you were created, till unrighteousness was found in you.

[16]In the abundance of your trade you were filled with violence in your midst, and you sinned; so I cast you as a profane thing from the mountain of God, and I destroyed you, O guardian cherub, from the midst of the stones of fire.

[17]Your heart was proud because of your beauty; you corrupted your wisdom for the sake of your splendour. I cast you to the ground: I exposed you before kings, to feast their eyes on you.

[18]By the multitude of your iniquities, in the unrighteousness of your trade you profaned your sanctuaries; so I brought fire out from your midst; it consumed you, and I turned you to ashes on the earth in the sight of all who saw you.

[19]All who know you among the peoples are appalled at you; you have come to a dreadful end and shall be no more for ever."

The Isaiah passage (*Isaiah 14:12-17*):

[12]"How you are fallen from heaven, O Day Star, son of Dawn! How you are cut down to the ground, you who laid the nations low!

[13]You said in your heart, 'I will ascend to heaven; above the stars of God I will set my throne on high; I will sit on the mount of assembly in the far reaches of the north;

[14]I will ascend above the heights of the clouds; I will make myself like the Most High.'

[15]But you are brought down to Sheol, to the far reaches of the pit.

[16]Those who see you will stare at you and ponder over you: 'Is this the man who made the earth tremble, who shook kingdoms.

[17]who made the world like a desert and overthrew its cities ...'

What do these passages reveal?

We learn from Isaiah that Satan was first named Lucifer, son of the morning. In Ezekiel we learn that he was created as a guardian cherub,[1] blameless in all his ways. He clearly had a high status as a created angelic being in God's heaven. He was perfect, beautiful and full of wisdom. He was adorned in precious stones, prepared for him on the day he was created.

He is described as being placed on the holy mountain of God and also that he was found in a Garden in Eden. It is not unreasonable to assume that this garden – let us call it the first Garden of Eden – was found on earth. Ezekiel goes on to say that Lucifer was blameless in all his ways.

Note that none of these attributes can be ascribed to the either king mentioned in the passages, the King of Babylon or the Prince of Tyre. Both of them were born in sin and were certainly not perfect - the King of Babylon is described as an oppressor, while the Prince of Tyre is described as proud.

What happened to Lucifer?

The short answer is: something terrible! Lucifer fell from grace by sinning. He rebelled against God! Ezekiel states that unrighteousness was found in him. He became proud, allowing his beauty and wisdom to corrupt him. Isaiah states that Lucifer said he would make himself like the Most High (i.e. like God). He would ascend to heaven above the angelic beings (stars of God) and set his throne there – either equal with or by displacing God.

In fact he rebelled and carried many angels with him. *Ezekiel 28:16-18* describes how he did this. The Hebrew word (richult)[2] usually translated *traffic, trade* or *merchandise*, more accurately means *to slander* or *gossip*. The passage means that Lucifer spoke against God to other angels and beings he ruled over on earth. This rebellion resulted in violence and lawlessness. We know that angels other than Lucifer have sinned, because Peter says that God did not spare the angels when they sinned, but cast them into hell to await judgement. (*2 Peter 2:4*).

The consequence of Lucifer's rebellion is that God cast him from the mountain of God. He has fallen from heaven. His ultimate fate is the Lake of Fire. *Matthew 24:41* says that hell has been created for the devil and his (fallen) angels. Meanwhile, as stated in the last chapter, it seems likely that God is allowing the devil a certain freedom to work his evil on earth so that the human race makes the choice either to follow God or stay under the authority of the devil.

Fallen angels

Many Christian writers believe that Satan carried a third of the angels with him in his rebellion against God. This figure is taken from Revelation where it says:

> The tail [of a great red dragon] swept down a third of the stars of heaven [angels] and cast them to earth.
>
> *(Revelation 12:4)*

There is no question that the dragon is Satan (see *Revelation 12:9*) and biblical teachers accept that the stars of heaven are angels. However, some writers believe that this capturing of a third of the angels is a future event, due to occur during the war in heaven between the archangel Michael and Satan, the dragon (see *Revelation 12:7-12*). The text does not make it clear. What we can say is that, besides the demons (see later), Satan has had fallen angels on his side throughout history.

These verses will illustrate the point:

> For we wrestle not against flesh and blood, but against principalities, against powers, against the rulers of the darkness of this world, against spiritual wickedness in high places.
>
> *(Ephesians 6:12 KJV)*

> He [Jesus] disarmed the rulers and authorities and put them to open shame, by triumphing over them in it [ie the Cross].[3]
>
> *(Colossians 2:15)*

> For God did not spare angels when they sinned, but cast them into hell [Tartarus] and committed them to chains of gloomy darkness to be kept until the judgement.
>
> *(2 Peter 2:4)*

> And the angels who did not stay within their own position of authority, but left their proper dwelling, he has kept in eternal chains under gloomy darkness until the judgement of the great

day – just as Sodom and Gomorrah and the surrounding cities, which likewise indulged in sexual immorality and pursued unnatural desire, serve as an example by undergoing a punishment of eternal fire.

(Jude 6-7)

*Then he [the Son of Man] will say to those on his left, "Depart from me, you cursed, into the eternal fire **prepared for the devil and his angels.**"*

(Matthew 24:41) [emphasis added]

*We know that we are from God, **and the whole earth lies under the power of the evil one**.*

(1 John 5:19) [emphasis added]

The prince of the kingdom of Persia withstood me twenty-one days, but Michael, one of the chief princes, came to help me.

(Daniel 10:13)

[This is the angel Gabriel speaking to Daniel, and mentioning that the archangel Michael came to his aid]

But now I will return to fight against the prince of Persia; and when I go out, behold, the prince of Greece will come . . . . there is none who contends by my side against these except Michael, your prince.

(Daniel 10:20-21)

[Here we see mention of two satanic spiritual princes who are contesting God's message to Daniel and mention too, that Michael is the prince of God's people Israel. It is worth reading *Daniel 10* and *12* to get the full picture].

These passages of scripture tell us a good deal about Satan and his kingdom of fallen angels. Some are operating in the heavenly places (mid-heaven) above the earth, while others, because of their particular sin, are already confined in a part of hell called Tartarus (*a Greek word in 2 Peter 2:4,*). When John says that the whole earth is under the power of the evil one it is clear that Satan is operating with an army of followers. He is a created being and would not have

61

the power to be everywhere at once. When God asks Satan what he has been doing (*Job 1:6-7*), Satan replied: *"from going to and fro on the earth, and from walking up and down on it."* He had clearly been keeping an eye on Job's righteousness before God.

The passages from Daniel also reveal that Satan's princes resist the work of God on earth, particularly in relation to his people Israel. Paul's passage from Ephesians introduces a new element into the relationship between Satan and the human race. Believers in Jesus are now able to challenge Satan: **to wrestle through prayer and intercession** with his evil purposes and bring change to humanity - the principal change being that people can be saved through the blood of Christ and thus transferred from Satan's kingdom of darkness to God's kingdom of light. The clear implication is that believers in Christ have an active part in achieving God's purposes on earth. This is all possible because of what Christ achieved on the Cross (*Colossians 2:15*).

Demonic Spirits

We now turn to the remaining group of spirits in Satan's kingdom of darkness. These are the demonic spirits.

Paul and the other New Testament writers rarely mention demons, but Jesus has a lot to say about them. A major part of his ministry was to set people free from the affliction of demons. Healing is often linked with the casting out of demons in the gospels. The gospel writer Mark says:

> *That evening at sundown, they brought to him all who were sick or oppressed with demons . . . . and he healed many who were sick with various diseases and cast out many demons.*
> *(Mark 1:32-34)*

> *And they [the disciples] cast out many demons, anointed with oil many who were sick and healed them.*
> *(Mark 6:13)*

We know from the gospels, and from experience of the deliverance ministry, that people can be troubled by demons, and in some situations they are even able to occupy or "possess" a human body. Jesus set people free from demons that were responsible for all manner of conditions. Among other conditions they were described as causing deafness, dumbness and blindness (*Matthew 12:22*) and epilepsy (*Matthew 12:16-18*).

Observations about demons from Jesus' ministry

1. They are invisible spirits often described as unclean, which roam around the earth.

2. They exist in large numbers. The Gadarene demoniac (possibly two demoniacs[4]), poor man, was possessed by a legion, in other words several thousand. When he was set free, the contrast in his personality was astonishing (*Mark 5:1-20*; in particular note *Mark 5:15*).

3. Demons recognised Jesus as the Son of God[5] and were afraid that he would send them to their eternal prison before their time was up (*Matthew 8:29; Luke 4:41*).

4. They are territorial. We can deduce this from the sequence of events whereby the Gadarene demoniac was set free. The demon who spoke to Jesus from the legion (using the man's voice), begged Jesus not to send the demons out of the country (i.e. the area adjacent to the Sea of Galilee) and instead to allow them to occupy a herd of swine feeding on the hillside. Jesus agreed to this (we will discuss why in a minute), but no sooner had the demons done so, the swine (numbering 2,000) rushed down the hill and drowned in the Sea of Galilee. This would have left the demons without a living body to occupy, as the pigs were now dead, but they were nevertheless still located in their assigned geographical area.

The question many believers ask is why did Jesus permit the demons to leave the man and then enter the swine, rather than just cast them out as he did in all other cases? One notices that many of the exorcisms were quite violent, even when carried out at the command of Jesus (*Mark 1:26; 9:26*). A popular explanation (with which I agree) is that Jesus recognised that the resistance to exit by so many demons might have damaged the Gadarene demoniac and so Jesus agreed they might enter

63

the swine to secure a quiet departure. Christians involved in modern-day exorcism often find that demons need to be expelled one by one.

5. Demons seek to occupy a physical body. This is not only deduced from the fact that Jesus expelled them from people. It is also apparent from Jesus' words in *Luke 11:*

> *When the unclean spirit has gone out of a person, it passes through waterless places seeking rest, and finding none it says, "I will return to my house from which I came." And when it comes, it finds the house swept and put in order. Then it goes and brings seven other spirits more evil than itself, and they enter and dwell there. And the last state of that person is worse than the first.*
> *(Luke 11:24-26)*

There are several things to note about this passage:

a) A demon calls a body its home and wants to dwell there.

b) A demon does not appear to like water. This possibly suggests that when demons were alive as beings, they were drowned in a flood. **However, I emphasise that this is supposition**, and not established fact!

c) Jesus was clearly indicating that when a person is set free from a demon(s) that they need to put something else in its place for fear of a re-invasion – that something else is faith in Christ himself and the Holy Spirit, who comes to dwell in a believer following their salvation.

6. Demons vary in strength. This is illustrated in a passage in the gospel of Mark (*Mark 9:17-29*) where a father brings his son with a dumb and deaf spirit to the disciples for deliverance and the disciples are unable to set the boy free. The behaviour of this demon is violent, causing strong physical manifestations so that the boy foams at the mouth, gnashes his teeth and throws himself into fire or water. When the father subsequently brings the boy to Jesus, Jesus rebukes the spirit which then

comes out of the boy by convulsing him violently as it does so. (Interestingly, in this passage Jesus tells the spirit never to enter the boy again).

The disciples later question Jesus as to why they did not succeed in casting out the demon. Jesus replies:

> *This kind cannot be driven out by anything but prayer [some manuscripts add: and fasting.]*
>
> *(Mark 9:29)*

7. Jesus refers to Satan's spiritual kingdom of darkness when some scribes accuse him of casting demons out by the power of Beelzebub, the prince of demons (*viz.* Satan). Jesus points out the illogicality of this view by saying:

> *How can Satan cast out Satan? If a kingdom is divided against itself, that kingdom cannot stand . . . . and if Satan has risen up against himself and is divided, he cannot stand, but is coming to an end.*
>
> *(see Mark 3:23-27)*

Jesus later goes on to explain that he casts out demons by the power of the Holy Spirit and that believers have been commissioned to do the same.

From these observations we see that Jesus himself has a lot to say about demons or unclean spirits, and he does it in a matter of fact and very business-like way. He would not want us to obsess over demons, but equally he wants his followers to accept their existence and extend the kingdom of God by dealing with them when appropriate.

There is a revealing passage in *Luke 10* when the seventy-two disciples return with joy, telling the Lord that even the demons are subject to them in his name. He then goes on to reiterate the authority he has given them, but says:

> *Nevertheless do not rejoice in this, that the spirits are subject to you, but rejoice that your names are written in heaven.*
>
> *(see Luke 10:17-20)*

Who or what are demons?

I have spent some time in this chapter discussing the nature of demons from a systematic review of Jesus' own words on the subject. I think Jesus' words and New Testament scripture generally distinguish between Satan's fallen angels and demonic spirits. Many Christian writers assume that demons are fallen angels and give little attention to whether this is a realistic explanation.

I contend that demonic spirits are not fallen angels. If this is true, then the next question has to be: what are they and where did they come from? The scriptures make clear that they are part of Satan's kingdom. They are disembodied spirits and the fact that they want to dwell in a body (preferably human) strongly suggests that they once occupied bodies.

Here are some possible answers

If one accepts that demons are not fallen angels, then there seem to be three possibilities:

a) They are human spirits awaiting the time of judgement. This is most unlikely since the Bible makes clear that at death unsaved human spirits descend into Hades (Sheol); in other words into hell. (*See Luke 16:19-31*).

b) They are the spirits of beings (giants) who came into existence from the illicit union of fallen angels with human women prior to the flood in Noah's time. These were hybrid human and angelic spirits. These unions are described in Genesis 6: they were hugely displeasing to God and were one of the reasons God chose to destroy the human race except for Noah and his family. These offspring were the Nephilim or Giants.

This is a possible explanation for the existence of demons, though one has to ask why human spirits would be consigned to hell at death while hybrid spirits were allowed to roam free. The flood would have led to the death of thousands, perhaps millions of human beings and whatever number of hybrid spirits were alive at that time.

c) The third possibility is that demons are the spirits of a pre-

Adamic race (or races) of beings who lived on earth in a pre-Adamic age. We cannot be sure of this, but we do know that there are a lot of these demonic spirits still free to roam the earth. As part of Satan's kingdom, their task is to afflict the human or Adamic race. We know from the story of the Gadarene demoniac that they will eventually be confined to hell, but for the time being they are free to exist on earth (see *Matthew 8:28-34* and *Luke 8:26-40*). We do not know why God has allowed them this latitude. My own view, **and this is supposition**, is that Satan and his angels had responsibility for a pre-Adamic earth along with any pre-Adamic races that may have lived on it. Satan sinned and fell from grace, taking the angels and the earth's inhabitants with him.

Why is Satan allowed to have continued access to the earth?

This is a reasonable question, and I will offer a possible explanation for why Satan, his angels and his demons continue to have access to the earth.

In view of the passages in Isaiah and Ezekiel (*Isaiah 14* and *Ezekiel 28*) concerning the fall of Lucifer, it is very possible that Adam was created to take over dominion of the earth from Satan. This would certainly have happened, had not Adam sinned by giving into the temptation of Satan in the Garden of Eden.

We notice in the story of Job how Satan was allowed to contest God's claims that Job was a righteous man (*Job 1* and *2*) and it seems very likely that in the same way he was allowed to challenge Adam's right to dominion over the earth. Satan failed with Job, but he did succeed with Adam.

However, the failure of Adam opened the way for God's own eternal Son to reclaim the situation in which Adam had landed the human race. What Adam failed to do, the Son Jesus Christ succeeded in doing. Adam gave into temptation, but Jesus resisted it. **Thus the way was opened for God finally to have a race of beings on earth who, once redeemed, were able to love him and not rebel.**

As we saw in Chapter 4, God operates according to legal principles. We can only surmise that God decided to use a fallen Satan to help in achieving his purposes. This he did by allowing Satan to challenge the Adamic race and not to have to vacate the earth until these purposes were achieved, according to God's legal principles. We saw in the passage from Colossians (*Colossians 2:14-15*) how Jesus' death on the Cross led to God's triumph over sin and the devil.

The fact that Satan and his fallen angels are still around in heavenly places, along with the demons confined to earth, is testimony to the fact that God is working out the redemption of the human race. He is allowing the human race to choose whether to remain under the authority of the devil or to accept God's offer of salvation. When this process is complete then Satan and all his angels and demons will finally be confined to hell.

This explanation may not be the correct one or it may not be correct in all its details, but to those readers who are sceptical, I would simply say: we cannot ignore the existence of these disembodied spirits. Demons must still be here on earth for a purpose. We know that God does not leave things to chance and the existence and function of demons cannot be outside of his purposes.

Visions beyond the Veil

Before we close this chapter I should like to draw the reader's attention to a book I came across forty years ago and which is still available. It is called *Visions beyond the Veil* by H.A. Baker and it describes Satan's kingdom along the lines I have just described from scripture.

Mr Baker and his wife were missionaries to China in the 1920s where they managed an orphanage for Chinese children. The orphanage experienced a powerful visitation by the Holy Spirit, where the Spirit spoke not to the adults, but to the children. For days on end the children had these visions and described them to their carers who wrote them down. They had visions of heaven and angels, of Jesus and his saving work and of Satan's kingdom. Many of the children were not yet believers, though many responded when they experienced these visions. Mr Baker diligently cross-referenced the visions with scripture. When I read and later re-read the book, I could find nothing which contradicted scripture[6].

Satan's kingdom was exactly as I have described it from the scriptures – a kingdom of quarrelsome powers in the heavenly places, quite different from the demons running around on earth.

The modern-day church's attitude to Satan

Much of the Church in the West has come to the liberal view that Satan is a metaphor for evil, and not a being in charge of a spiritual kingdom. *Visions beyond the Veil* and the experience of Christians in pagan cultures give the lie to this outlook. Believers in Africa, for example, have no difficulty in accepting these scriptural truths, because they will be familiar with evil spirits in their communities. Witchcraft is prevalent and witch doctors have real spiritual power over people. For the Church in the West to be really effective in ministering Christ to the people, it needs to acknowledge the reality of Satan and his kingdom.

Conclusion

This chapter has explored how Lucifer came to be Satan, God's adversary, and how he rules over a kingdom of spiritual darkness. This kingdom is populated by fallen angels or satanic princes and rulers who dwell in the mid-heaven (heavenly places), along with a host of demonic spirits who dwell on earth.

Because of the sin of Adam and Eve it is important to understand that human beings also belong in Satan's kingdom of darkness. The human race was taken captive by Satan way back in the Garden of Eden. However, God has given us the opportunity to escape from Satan's kingdom when we accept Jesus Christ as our Saviour and Lord.

NOTES

1. **Angelic beings**: The Bible mentions angels many times but does not say much about their classification or hierarchy. The first distinction is between holy angels and fallen angels. We examine the existence and hierarchy of fallen angels in this chapter, so this note is about the holy angels, those who remained faithful to God. If we take the word angel as a generic name for spiritual beings in heaven then we have archangels, cherubim, seraphim and angels.

   Angels have many functions, but in overall terms they are described as: "ministering spirits sent out to serve for the sake of those who are to inherit salvation." *(Hebrews 1:14)*. Michael is the only angel described as an archangel *(Jude 9)* but many writers believe that Gabriel is also an archangel. Scripture does not mention other archangels by name, but the apocryphal book, Tobit, mentions Raphael as one of the seven archangels. We cannot take this as fact, but Gabriel describes Michael as one of the chief princes *(Daniel 10:13)*, so it is possible that there are other archangels. The term prince is also used of satanic princes such as the prince of Persia *(Daniel 10:13, 20)*.

   Cherubim and seraphim seem to be angels with special duties before God the Father. (Satan was described as a cherub before he rebelled.) Cherubim are mentioned many times in scripture. They seem to be angels with the special role of praising and worshipping God and exercising his power *(Genesis 3:24)*. They have four wings: two to cover their body and two for flying. Images of two cherubim were created to cover the Ark of God in the Tabernacle in the wilderness. Seraphim (fiery, burning ones) are only mentioned by name once in the Bible *(Isaiah 6:2-4)*. They appear to be angels who worship God continually. They also seem to serve as angels of purification, as one placed a burning coal on Isaiah's lips which took away his guilt and atoned for his sin. They have six wings: they use two to cover their face, two to cover their feet and two to fly.

2. It is important to be clear that the phrase used in verse 16 to describe Satan's activities is derived from the Hebrew verb *Le'rachel* which means *to gossip or peddle*. The Hebrew phrase used in the text is *richultach*, which literally means *your gossip*.

3. I generally refer to the principal fallen angels in Satan's kingdom as **principalities** and **powers**, the words used in the King James Version of the Bible. However, other translations use terms such as rulers and authorities. I go into more detail about the hierarchy of Satan's kingdom in Chapter 14. I have used the English Standard Version for this verse from Colossians as it is better understood than the King James Version.

4. It is worth noting that while Matthew refers to two demoniacs, Mark and Luke only refer to one. The narrative suggests that all three are describing the same incident, but the discrepancy does not present an insurmountable problem. There are likely to have been two demoniacs (otherwise Matthew's facts are wrong), but it is likely that one was more prominent and therefore picked out by Mark and Luke. Most people have had the experience whereby they have had a conversation with more than one person, but one person was more dominant or noticeable and over time this is the person they come to remember. This is certainly **not** an example which could be used to deny the reliability of scripture.

5. The fact that demons recognised Jesus as the Son of God is hugely significant. They also recognised and were fearful of his power. Human beings over the centuries have written tomes about whether God exists and whether Jesus was God or even existed as an historical figure. Humans may doubt, but demons as spiritual beings do not! They know! It is an uncomfortable fact, but the existence of the devil and his kingdom is among the strongest evidence for the existence of God and his eternal Son, Jesus Christ. The peoples of Africa, India, China and South America are well aware of the existence of spirits. Sadly they often worship them. Christians who serve in these countries are also aware of them, as are Christians in the Western world who are called to minister and set people free from demonic bondage. It is only the secular West who thinks this talk of demons is primitive claptrap. This has been one of Satan's most successful strategies in modern times: he has persuaded modern, secular and scientific man that he and his spirits do not exist. Christians in the Western churches need to be aware of this deception.

6. I think that *Visions beyond the Veil* is a wonderful Holy Spirit-inspired book. I have just one small observation which is that the visions do

not seem to distinguish between Hades, the place where the unsaved dead go prior to the Judgement at the Great White Throne (*Revelation 20:11-15*) and the Lake of Fire, where they go after the Judgement. The Lake of Fire is described as the second death (*Revelation 20:6, 14-15*) and so must be distinct from Hades, the place of the dead prior to judgement. It is a small point, and it may be that the Holy Spirit decided not to overload the children with such distinctions. The most important fact is that the Lake of Fire is unsaved humanity's final destination. This is made fully clear in the children's visions. (*This book is still available from Freedom Publishing.*)

Chapter 6
Satan's Activities among the Human Race (Part 1)

The next two chapters are devoted to describing Satan's activities among the human race.

At the start of this discourse I need to remind the reader that God holds each human being accountable for the sins they commit. He never accepts the excuse "the devil made me do it!" However, our nature of sin gives Satan a foothold in every human life and these chapters will illustrate that he makes good use of it!

We saw in Chapter 4 that Satan still retains control over the kingdoms of the human race. In this chapter we are going to examine the way in which Satan exerts this control. The world and the Church are woefully unaware of the extent of his influence and activities. Most Christians do not realise the extent of Satan's penetration into society and the lives of individual people. As people have turned away from the Christian faith of our forefathers, Satan has moved in to fill the gap. In Western society the media, music and culture has been a target for Satan, particularly among the young. All these activities are motivated by a hatred of God and of the human race, which was originally made in God's image. In *John 8* Jesus has some harsh words to say to the Jews who were seeking to kill him:

> *You are of your father the devil, and your will is to do your father's desires. He was a murderer from the beginning, and he has nothing to do with the truth, because there is no truth in him. When he lies, he speaks out of his own character, for he is a liar and the father of lies.*
>
> *(John 8:44)*

In a later passage Jesus alludes to the devil when he says:

The thief comes only to steal and kill and destroy.

(John 10:10)

The word Satan means **adversary** and he is described as the "accuser of the brethren" (*Revelation 12:10*). It seems that he still has access to God[1] where he accuses believers of their sins, despite believers having been forgiven through the shed blood of Christ.

The consequences for human history

With this catalogue of Satan's evil intent, it is not surprising that the history of the human race has been anything but peaceful. Strife and wars have dominated history. Clearly a powerful, invisible force has been in existence to take advantage of the sinful nature and motivate humanity to do evil.

How is it that so many human beings long for peace only to find that war flares up in one corner of the earth and then in another? In terms of numbers, the twentieth century has been the worst century in history for death and destruction. The two world wars wrought immense destruction and cost millions of lives. The First World War was hopefully described as 'the war to end all wars', but within twenty years we were into the even more destructive Second World War. Since then, as nations have sought to escape colonial empires, there has been one war after another somewhere on the globe. All these activities are primed and stirred up by Satan and his army of fallen angels and demonic spirits.

If we want a more direct example of Satan's intervention in human affairs, we only have to look at the Holocaust of World War II. What on earth motivated a group of leaders in a modern western state (Germany) with a background of science and culture, to initiate the extermination of a whole race of people, the Jews? It is beyond belief, but it happened! By the end of World War II, the Nazis had murdered six million Jews and other citizens they considered undesirable. What motivated the Russia of Stalin and the China of Mao Zedong to kill millions of their own people?

These terrible acts were motivated by a malevolent spirit! Some people believe that all human beings could commit such evil acts, if pushed to the limit. That may or may not be true, but what this outlook omits is the powerful influence of an invisible, helping hand; the hand of Satan.

Satan's intentions

Satan seeks to achieve three principal objectives:

A. To ruin God's image as found in the human race (*Genesis 1:26*).
B. To thwart God's purposes for reconciling the human race to himself through belief in Jesus Christ and what Jesus did on the Cross.
C. To direct human worship towards himself in place of worship rightly belonging to God, or to cause people to become atheists.

In order to understand how Satan operates we need first to examine the moral laws given directly by God to Moses on Mount Sinai for the Jewish people, and by extension the whole of humanity. These moral laws are the Ten Commandments (the Decalogue) and they provide an overarching set of rules by which people should live, relate to each other and relate to God himself.

Here are the Commandments paraphrased:

1. You shall have no other gods besides me.

2. You shall not make for yourself a carved image as something to bow down to worship.

3. You shall not take the name of the Lord your God in vain.

4. You are to remember the Sabbath day and keep it holy.

5. Honour your father and your mother.

6. You shall not murder.

7. You shall not commit adultery

8. You shall not steal

9. You shall not lie (bear false witness).

10. You shall not covet or be envious of other people's possessions.

These ten commandments were expanded and illustrated in the remainder of the Mosaic Law. In New Testament times Jesus interpreted the Commandments in two ways. He made some of them more exacting, but he also displayed mercy and reconciliation in the operation of the laws. For example, in the Sermon on the Mount (*Matthew 5*) Jesus compares anger[2] to murder and lust to adultery, but elsewhere he talks about being reconciled to one's brother and he forgives the woman caught in adultery, telling her to sin no more (*John 8:1-11*). Interestingly, no mention is made of the man caught in adultery. Perhaps Jesus wanted to draw attention to the man's involvement, when he said to the assembled men: "Let him who is without sin among you be the first to throw a stone at her".

The ten commandments are important, not only because they provide absolute standards of behaviour, but because Satan has sought to overturn them and persuade people to live by different values.

Satan damages the image of God when he causes people to break these rules. As mentioned earlier, Satan cannot attack God directly, but he tries to do this by defacing his image in sinful man in a whole number of ways.

Satan thwarts God's plans for reconciling the human race to himself when he deflects people away from knowledge of Jesus and the conviction of sin by the Holy Spirit. He points them towards idolatry and ultimately worship of himself. In doing this he causes people to move away from worshipping God, thus leading them to disobey Commandments 1 and 2.

Foundational truths of Church belief

As well as undermining the Ten Commandments, Satan has also subtly undermined the biblical beliefs of the Church. In modern times this commenced with what was called 'Higher Criticism' by theologians which began towards the end of the nineteenth century and flourished in the early twentieth century.

The foundational beliefs of scripture, especially the New Testament, were undermined by the view that scripture did not have to be taken literally. The miraculous conception of Jesus, the miracles in the Gospels, the resurrection of Jesus were all challenged. The amazing discoveries of modern science were used to argue that the miraculous was an invention of the human mind to explain seemingly difficult things and that they had not happened as described in the Bible.

Higher Criticism came into popular view in the 1960s with Bishop John Robinson's book *Honest to God* with the implication that God as 'the ground of our being' was in everything. Sin, the need for repentance and the new birth in Christ fell by the wayside.

God is love and the judgemental side of God's character was set aside. This later led to a loosening of God's moral laws, as the yardstick became God's love and not his abhorrence of sin.

In modern times this has led to the acceptance of social and moral behaviours that are quite contrary to scripture: alternative lifestyles, human rights displacing God's rights and laws. Values are either considered to be relative or to be underpinned by universal human rights.

The Ten Commandments

I do not intend to make a detailed description of the Ten Commandments as this may distract from the purpose of the book which is how to tackle Satan and his evil influence. However, I will spend some time on Commandments 1 and 2 as disobeying these serves to defy God who is the only being to be worshipped. In the following chapter I will look at some of the other ways in which Satan has sought to deflect the human race away from God's desires and commands and has succeeded in blinding people to the truth. This has very serious consequences for humanity.

Commandments 1 and 2:
You shall have no other gods beside me or worship any carved images

This has been the devil's principal realm of activity. From early in history Satan has persuaded people to worship him, but usually in a disguised form. The Law was given to Moses and the Israelites as they were about to enter the Promised Land – a land occupied by many pagan tribes. One of the reasons God purposed to destroy or drive out the tribes was because they worshipped foreign gods like Baal, Molech and Ashtoreth. As they worshipped these gods they indulged in depraved and abominable practices such as cult prostitution and human sacrifice. The practice particularly offensive to God was the sacrifice of children to Molech, by burning them in fire (see *Leviticus 18:21; 20:2-4; Jeremiah 32:35*). They also carved images of these gods in stone, wood or metal, often taking an animal or human form. At other times they worshipped the sun, moon, and stars.

Of course, these were not real gods; they were a cover for Satan and his demons. This is clear from several passages, which forbid making sacrifices to demons (*Leviticus 17:7; Deuteronomy 32:17*):

> *[Israel] stirred him [God] to jealousy with strange gods, with abominations they provoked him to anger. They sacrificed to demons that were no gods, to gods they had never known . . . . and you forgot the God who gave you birth.*
>
> *(Deuteronomy 32:16-18)*

As this passage reveals, Satan was successful in seducing the Israelites to follow after the pagan gods of their predecessors in the land. In the New Testament, the apostle Paul is talking about food sacrificed to idols when he writes:

> *What do I imply then? . . . . I imply that what pagans sacrifice they offer to demons and not to God. I do not want you to be participants with demons.*
>
> *(1 Corinthians 10:19-20)*

In Revelation we find these words:

> *The rest of mankind, who were not killed by these plagues, did not repent of the works of their hands, **nor give up worshipping demons** and idols of gold and silver and bronze and stone or wood which cannot see or hear or walk.*
>
> *(Revelation 9:20)* [emphasis added]

How does this relate to today's world?

It is easy today to think that these admonitions apply to a more primitive epoch in human history. As a school pupil I found the idea that people would worship idols very strange. What was the point in worshipping a piece of wood or stone carved to look like a man or something in nature? It seemed plain foolishness, but what I did not know then, and for many years later, was the spiritual force behind these images. These forces are still at work. Many peoples in different parts of the world still worship elemental spirits. They know that these evil spirits are real and that they can cause harm, and so worship them, and ceremonial rites become ways to appease and placate these spirits.

Many people in Western societies, where society is undergirded by a rational, scientific approach to life, think this kind of idolatry is primitive nonsense. They make a great mistake: Satan is the master of deception (*2 Corinthians 11:14*). Following the scientific or rational enlightenment of the eighteenth and nineteenth centuries, Satan has moved on. He causes people to dispense with God and rely on human thinking, human activities (e.g. sport) or material things. People do not recognise an obsession with material things as a form of idolatry.

Alternatively, Satan appeals to man's inborn spiritual needs by persuading people to follow other religions, Christian cults or less well-defined spiritual activities such as Eastern meditation. Think of the many people who have a statue of Buddha in their home!

Where Satan can persuade people to practise more ancient idolatry, he continues to use witch doctors, shamans or witches. But where this is no longer possible, he introduces other forms of idolatry. At its most extreme Satan may succeed in persuading people to worship him directly as in Satanism. However, it is much more likely that he will be worshipped indirectly under an alternative name. Secret societies and cults such as Freemasonry are riddled with pagan beliefs and practices. They may claim to believe in God, but this is a cover for pagan worship. Masonry accepts members from every religion and contends that the holy books and deities of these religions are of equal status – presenting an obvious contradiction[3].

The true God is only reached through Jesus Christ

The sad fact is that every other spiritual activity is a deflection from the one true and only faith, salvation in Jesus Christ. Scripture is abundantly clear about this:

There is salvation in no one else [Jesus], for there is no other name under heaven given among men by which we must be saved.

(Acts 4:12)

For there is one God and there is one mediator between God and men, the man Christ Jesus, who gave himself as a ransom for all.

(1 Timothy 2:5-6)

Many Christians are simply unaware that activities derived from Eastern meditation, such as yoga, are spiritually unsound and should be avoided. Other Christians think that all religions aspire to reach the same god and are therefore in favour of inter-faith activities, but this is contrary to scripture. The god of Islam and the gods of Eastern religions are not the same as the God of Judaism and Christianity and we should not interact with these faiths at a spiritual level.

Some churches, especially in the Anglican community, are now hosting interfaith meetings where they invite representatives of religions such as Islam, and Eastern religions to participate in services and even to preach from their pulpits. It is ironical given that no imam would ever invite a Christian minister to preach on salvation through Jesus Christ in one of their mosques![4]

The Sanctity of God's word

Jesus said that the path to destruction is broad, while the path to eternal life is narrow (*Matthew 7:13-14*). We are required to follow this narrow path and stick to what scripture permits. This is why it is so important to recognise that scripture; the Old and New Testaments, is the final written Word of God. Human additions or modifications to scripture such as we find in the Latter Day Saints (Mormons), Jehovah's Witnesses and Christian Science are not permitted.

Many scriptures from the Bible attest to this fact. Here are a few:

You shall not add to the word which I command you, nor take from it . . . .

(Deuteronomy 4:2)

Every word of God proves true . . . . do not add to his words, lest he rebuke you . . . .

(Proverbs 30:5-6)

Scripture cannot be broken.

(John 10:35)

But, even if we, or an angel from heaven, should preach to you a gospel contrary to that which we preached to you, let him be accursed.

(Galatians 1:8)

Satan's never-ending objective

We need to remember that today, as well as throughout history, Satan has sought to deflect the human race from the worship of the one true God. Sometimes Satan has sought to cause man to exalt himself in the place of God, such as the worship of great leaders or human achievements,[5] but at other times he has sought to have man worship Satan's invisible kingdom. It has made no difference whether people have realised this or not: scripture reveals that idol worship is the worship of demonic spirits.

There will come a time in history, just before Jesus Christ returns to earth, when Satan will be directly worshipped through his final human agent, the **Antichrist**. God will allow this manifestation of Satan and his power to demonstrate the bankrupt and sinful nature of Satan's kingdom and his rebellion against God. It will also demonstrate the rebellion of the human race in these last days before Christ's glorious return to earth.

NOTES

1. It may seem strange that Satan still has access to God, but we know that this was true at the time of Job, and we also know that it is true in the New Testament. *Revelation 12:10* says the devil accuses believers day and night before God, until he is cast down to earth. Scripture also says the Lord Jesus makes intercession for the Saints before the Father in heaven *(Romans 8:34; Hebrews 7:25)*. I will elaborate on this in Chapter 17 when discussing Satan's opposition to the Church.

2. *You have heard that it was said to those of old, "you shall not murder; and whoever murders will be liable to judgement." But I say to you that everyone who is angry with his brother will be liable to judgement.*

    (Jesus speaking in Matthew 5:21-22).

    You have heard that it was said, "you shall not commit adultery," but I say to you that everyone who looks at a woman with lustful intent has already committed adultery with her in his heart.

    (Matthew 5:27-28)

3. Christians need to beware of all secret societies, not least Freemasonry. For many years Masonry was able to keep its secrets, because members swear oaths that would bring terrible consequences if they broke their silence. Over the last half century much knowledge has come to light, either because the masons are more open, or because people have left and described the oaths and practices. Members who have left and come to a personal faith in Christ have also spoken out. At the lower degrees, particularly the first three, leading to Master Mason, members believe in the Great Architect of the Universe (GAOTU), but at higher degrees members are given the real name of their god which is JAHBULON. This god is a composite of JAH (Yahweh or Jehovah), BUL or Baal, the major god of the Canaanites in biblical times, and ON or Osiris, the Egyptian god of the underworld. A moment's reflection on what Moses had to say about idol worship and Canaanite gods makes it abundantly clear that our God (the Old Testament Yahweh) will not for a minute countenance such a composite deity.

    There is much literature on this subject by Christians and also ministries such as Sozo Ministries International who specialise in setting people free from the spiritual ties incurred by membership of such cults. *Unmasking Freemasonry (Removing the Hoodwink)* by *Selwyn Stevens* is a good introductory book.

4. York Minster (second in the hierarchy of Anglican churches) was in the news in the summer of 2019 for allowing the practice of Zen-Buddhist meditation in the cathedral grounds. It was set up by one of its senior clergy who is a believer in 'dual religious belonging' the idea that people can have a foot in more than one religious camp – in this instance that Christians can benefit from Zen meditation. This is one of the Eastern meditations where one "empties one's mind" to allow random thoughts to enter; a dangerous spiritual practice and very different from Christian meditation on God's Word. Such meditation is dangerous because it opens the door to demonic influence. Fortunately. It looks as though the new dean to the cathedral is going to stop this practice.

5. The twentieth century has several examples of leaders who exalted themselves to godlike status or who were subject to adulation by their people – men like Hitler, Mussolini, Stalin and Mao Zedong come to mind. The New Testament has a salutary example of the more direct consequences of such adulation. In the book of Acts (*Acts 12:20-23*), King Herod allowed himself to be worshipped as a god, but was struck dead by an angel and eaten by worms!

Chapter 7
Satan's Activities among the Human Race (Part 2)

A. SATANIC STRONGHOLDS

The apostle Paul has a well-known verse in *2 Corinthians*:

> For though we walk in the flesh, we are not waging war
> according to the flesh. For the weapons of our warfare are not
> of the flesh, but have divine power to destroy strongholds.
> *(2 Corinthians 10:3-4)*

This verse encourages us to believe that we can defeat these
strongholds and thus defeat Satan, a subject we come to in Part
II of the book. In this chapter we will examine conditions where
such strongholds operate. They may be responsible for illness,
addictions and compulsions. I shall also say something more about
Satanism, witchcraft and curses.

Sins of the fathers

Many Christians are not aware that they can be entrapped by Satan
through things that happened even before they were born. The
source of this knowledge is a passage of scripture following the First
and Second Commandments in Exodus in which God specifically
forbids idolatry:

> You shall have no other gods before me. You shall not make for
> yourself a carved image . . . . you shall not bow down to them
> or serve them . . . .
> *(Exodus 20:3-5)*

The text goes on to say:

For I the Lord your God am a jealous God, visiting iniquity of the fathers on the children to the third and fourth generation of those who hate me.

However, this very sombre statement is immediately followed by:

but showing steadfast love to thousands of those who love me and keep my commandments.
(Exodus 20:5-6)

We thus see two streams: one of cursing and one of blessing. Most of us are familiar with families where the family seems to be under a curse: excessive illness, addictive behaviours, and unnatural deaths. One family where there is an alleged curse is the Kennedy family in America, which has had an unusually high level of misfortune, including death. The most well-known of these incidents, was the tragic assassination of President John Kennedy in 1963. Such tragedies do not establish a spiritual dimension in itself, but it does cause people to wonder[1].

On the other hand, we may know of families that seem to be blessed with minimal illness, longevity and success in life. I believe this difference between cursing and blessing stems from Commandments 1 & 2. A blessed family may be one where forebears such as grandparents or great grandparents were fine upstanding believers in Christ and the blessing has trickled down the generational line to descendants who may no longer be especially faithful or religious.

Where the first two Commandments have been severely disobeyed, a person or their family may have become vulnerable to attack by Satan leading to the curse of illness or other misfortunes. Sadly, it is a neglected spiritual principle but failure to stay within God's parameters for worship and behaviour opens us up to attack by Satan.

Satanism and witchcraft

We have already spoken of idolatry in relation to Commandments 1 and 2. An extreme form of idolatry is the **direct worship of Satan** in Satanism and witchcraft[2]. Both acknowledge Satan, both invoke the power of demons and both indulge in satanic practices, often involving sex. Their involvement with the occult is such that they can exercise real spiritual power, often through cursing people. People are rightly fearful of witch doctors and shamans because of their occult power to harm people through curses.

Humanists, who think that science and the age of enlightenment have exposed the occult as primitive superstition, are living in a fool's paradise. People who live among witch doctors and shamans know they have real spiritual power.

The commandment against idolatry is very clear and we cannot expect God to protect us if we take such a step into spiritual darkness.

Health

Health is a major area where Satan afflicts people with trouble. Not all health problems can be attributed to the devil. Many illnesses and diseases are a consequence of the original fall of the human race through Adam and Eve. We know that Satan can afflict people with disease because of what God permitted him to do to Job (*Job 1 and 2*). We also know that Jesus set people free from illness, some of which was caused by demons, but some of which were due to natural causes.

What we know from modern-day Christian ministry is that sinful attitudes and practices can often give Satan leverage in our lives. **Forgiveness** is perhaps the major issue here. Jesus makes it clear that it is absolutely essential to forgive those who have wronged us, however long ago the incident happened. Christian counsellors find that mental conditions and physical disabilities disappear when people are able to face the hurt in their lives and to forgive the person(s) responsible.

Another significant factor is the inheritance by children of the consequences of the sins of their parents and forefathers. This seems a harsh consequence, but God clearly states in *Exodus 20* that when people break the First and Second Commandments and practise idolatry, God will visit their iniquity on the children to the third and fourth generations (*Exodus 20:3-6*). He says he will do this because he is a jealous God, jealous when the Israelites (and by implication the whole of humanity) play the harlot and go after other gods.

When this happens, Satan gets a foothold in a family's life and can cause demonic oppression, disability and sickness. The good news is that no satanic power can defeat the power of Jesus to save and to heal. There are many stories of people who have been delivered from the effects of involvement with the occult. Sometimes children are inducted by their families to become mediums for spirit guides, long before they are able to make up their own minds[3].

Sometimes Satanism masquerades as a church in the so-called Spiritualist churches, where there may be lip service to the Bible, but never to Jesus. A principal activity at such groups is the medium who allegedly puts people in touch with dead relatives. The relatives are none other than demonic spirit guides.

Addictions

These are a plague of modern society. Countless numbers of lives have been ruined by drugs and alcohol addiction. The misuse of alcohol has happened throughout history, but the widespread use of drugs took off in Western society during the liberalisation of the 1960s. Drug abuse has now reached epidemic proportions.

Here, Satan encourages people to try something which then causes a physiological change in the body, especially the brain, which leads to addiction. This physiological change to the body's cells makes it really difficult to break the addiction. Interestingly, it has also been shown that repeated exposure to pornography has a similar physiological effect, even though the stimulus is visual and not chemical. This is why it is so hard for people (both men and women) to break the pornographic habit[4]. These addictions are all used by Satan to deface the image of God in a human being, often leading to the break-up of marriages and families and even to death. Gambling is another devastating addiction leading to loss of jobs, loss of homes and family break-up.

Compulsions

This word is used to describe activities like inveterate lying or stealing. Initially, lying or stealing are a consequence of man's sinful nature. When, however, we meet a compulsion to do this we can be reasonably sure that the person is motivated by a demon.

B. CHANGES IN BEHAVIOUR IN THE TWENTIETH CENTURY

It would no doubt surprise our forefathers to see what has become acceptable behaviour in modern Western societies. Even as recently as my own childhood, Christian values undergirded how people behaved and such values were still taught to children at school.

This was particularly true around sexual morality and I well remember that young men who got their girlfriends pregnant were expected to marry them. Society disapproved of alternative lifestyles and the killing of unborn babies. Before I look further at Satan's attack on God's standards in this area, I want to explain the significance of marriage between a man and a woman in God's eyes.

Marriage is a covenant before God

The significance of marriage between a man and a woman is that it is a covenant between themselves and with God. Covenants before God are very serious matters. He has made several covenants with the human race or with individuals and he will never break them. He made a covenant with Abraham to make a race of his descendants, the Jewish people, from whom the Messiah would come as the Saviour of humanity. God confirmed this covenant with both Isaac, Abraham's son, and Jacob his grandson, so that there could be no misunderstanding as to whom it applied. It is this covenant which makes us confident that God is working out his purposes (stated in the Bible) in bringing the Jewish people back to their ancient land, the land of Israel.

God also made a personal covenant with King David to say that there would always be someone to sit on his throne (*2 Samuel 7*). We now know that the ultimate king in this line of David is King Jesus who will reign from Jerusalem when he returns to earth.

Returning to the covenant of marriage we find in the Old Testament that God looks upon the Israelites, the Jewish nation, as a wife – he is betrothed to them. This may seem a strange concept, but we are talking about our infinite God, so what is not possible for us as individuals can be possible to God. He was very jealous when the Israelites went after other (Satanic) gods in the form of idolatry. He even contemplated divorcing them (*Jeremiah 3:8*), but because he had made this contract, he remained faithful to them.

Marriage and its associated sexual union are special to God

The covenant of marriage explains why marriage and the sexual union between a man and wife are so special to God. He has put a special mark on it by making it the means whereby a man and woman can create new life. They provide the fertilised embryo, while God adds the child's spirit (*Zechariah 12:1*). It also helps to explain why, despite the pressure against marriage, it still proves to be highly popular across all faiths, not just the Christian and Jewish faiths.

However, it also explains why marriage has been such a target for Satan. He has encouraged people to break Commandment 7 (*You shall not commit adultery*) and tackled the destruction of marriage in a number of ways:

1. He targets marriage to break it up. Many Christians can testify to this fact whether they have succumbed to the pressures or successfully resisted them. It has come to light that witches' covens are known to pray against Christian marriages.

2. He tempts people to unfaithfulness. Christian ministers in particular need to guard their marriages.

3. He puts couples under pressure through physical and mental abuse, usually, but not always the man abusing the wife.

4. He encourages couples to live together rather than marry.

5. He encourages single parent families through sexual irresponsibility, usually by the father. (*I am not of course referring to single parent families where the remaining parent has to bring up the family through death or desertion of the other parent*).

Other areas of concern

Western society has now largely accepted a lax attitude towards marriage, the acceptance of divorce, alternative lifestyles and the abortion of the unborn child. There are however two further subjects, which are different in that they do not meet with the approval of society. These are violence towards women and child sexual abuse. However, it is not difficult to see the hand of Satan at work here.

Pornography and a lax attitude towards sex have led young men to a sense of entitlement towards women; violence and rape do not carry the taboo they once did. Society disapproves but has been singularly unsuccessful in stopping the spread of such immoral attitudes and behaviour. It might have been more successful if it had taken a stronger attitude towards the spread of pornography.

There is too, genuine horror in society at the extent of child abuse; and the law now takes a severe approach to the punishment of paedophiles. One of the shocking discoveries has been the extent of child abuse in the churches, both catholic and protestant, for decades. For many years this was covered up but is now getting proper exposure.

The need to recognise God's judgement of sin as well as his love for people

I want to return to the subject of alternative lifestyles (LGBTQ+)[5] and to abortion. These are contentious subjects even among Christians and I want to start by saying that in the past there were bad things about the attitude of society towards homosexuals and young women seeking abortions. For people who found themselves with same sex attraction or women who found themselves expecting a baby, society could be very harsh. Among Christians there could be a lack of God's love which needed to be held in balance with the recognition of sin and the fact that God's laws were being broken. Too often the attitude was one of condemnation without the love of God. A famous case of ostracism and persecution of homosexuals was the brilliant mathematician Alan Turing, who sadly took his own life in 1954. Let us be quite clear that this persecution and lack of love is wrong.

Abortion has now reached epidemic proportions, but it would be unfair not to recognise that many young women are vulnerable and find themselves in a position where they have conceived and do not know how to handle the forthcoming pregnancy[6]. Likewise, there are difficult situations where if doctors know that either the mother or the foetus will die, whom do they save?[7] However, these situations are very different to the acceptance of abortion as a legitimate exercise of womens' rights. The elevation of these rights in recent times denies the right of life to the unborn child and God's role in its creation (see *Psalm 139:13-14; Zechariah 12:1*)

Consequences of the sexual revolution of the 1960s

The problem with the sexual and social revolution of the 1960s was that while harsh attitudes were jettisoned (a good thing) sinful behaviour was sanctioned. This has had consequences that few people could foresee at the time. Today, fifty years later, we have a society which sanctions gay marriage, approves of same sex activity and condones abortion of the unborn child.

I know that Christian opinion is divided on these issues: some approving, some neutral and some disapproving. Those who disapprove believe the Bible teaches that marriage should be between a man and a woman (heterosexual), that divorce is a breakdown of what should be a lifelong commitment and that abortion is the killing of an unborn child. (See Jesus' views on marriage and divorce: *Matthew 19:4-6; Mark 10:7-9*)

Satan's role in the changing morals of society

I believe that Satan has helped to engineer this acceptance among Christians of things contrary to the will of God. He has done this by persuading people to ignore the judgemental side of God's character. His theme has been along the seductive line that "if two people love each other", then it does not matter that this love is between two men or two women. "Love trumps all!" The alternative tactic is to emphasise universal human rights. A woman has rights over her own body and therefore the right not to continue with an unwanted pregnancy. This deception fails to ask the question: "Does the unborn child not have the right to life?"

Furthermore, if God is the author of life, which the Bible clearly states that he is (see previous section), then does he not have rights to the lives he has created? If that is true, then the whole matter of human rights must be framed within the context of God's creation and not simply what people think at any stage of history.

I am not against rights which accord with God's laws. This is why for mankind with its fallen nature, a modern democratic society is the best form of government. It allows checks and balances and freedom of expression which dictatorships do not.

In my opinion Satan has succeeded in undermining the truths of the Bible. This is why it is so important that Christians should understand and stick to the Word of God. To subscribe to the parts of the Bible one likes, but to set aside parts one does not like, is a quick way to fall into biblical error.

To take a biblical stance on moral issues does not mean that one has to be harsh or to take an unloving attitude towards people, or to zoom in on particular sins as though they are worse than others. The Bible is clear that all people have sinned as the following verses make clear (*Romans 3:23, 5:12; Ecclesiastes 7:20; 1 Kings 8:46*).

Christians are now on the wrong side of prevailing values in Western countries

One of the problems for Christians today is that the turnaround of moral attitudes over the last sixty years has meant that Christians and Christian values are no longer mainstream: Christians now find themselves on the outside of society with the ever-increasing risk that they will be persecuted by the state or zealous citizens, for publicly declaring their faith and what the Bible teaches. This is a sorry state of affairs and one which has happened relatively quickly since the so-called sexual revolution of the 1960s.

Another area where Christians are being squeezed is around alternative religions, together with the "woke" movement. Islam is the principal religion where this has happened. In the last twenty years there has been a concerted effort by Islamic leaders to label anything which is critical of Islam as 'Islamaphobic'. It is ironical that when I was a young man, blasphemy laws protected the Christian faith. Today these have been abolished. Few people other than Christians care about whether the Lord's name is taken in vain. However, anything that is critical of Islam or the prophet Mohammed is immediately pounced upon as an affront to the Muslim faith; it is deemed Islamaphobic.

Although the State no longer has blasphemy laws, it does have laws which forbid people from being offensive over race, religion and lifestyle, where a person can be prosecuted simply for saying something which might offend a particular group of people. This is very different from prosecuting people for saying things which might incite people to racial or other types of violence. There is clear evidence that certain people are determined to use these laws against Christians for expressing biblical views on alternative lifestyles. Christians are put on the defensive in a democratic and traditionally Christian society where discussion and the expression of opposing views should be taken as the sign of a healthy and tolerant society.

'No-platforming' and the 'woke' movement

The 'woke'[8] movement has taken this even further. People, particularly students, are to be protected from views which might offend or upset them. The result is that speakers find they are 'no-platformed'. Invitations to speak are rescinded or not given, because their views differ from the prevailing view on 'sensitive topics' within religion, race and sex. This may be done through the Student Union or the university authorities themselves. Some university departments have taken to attaching warnings to reading lists where literature, traditionally valued as essential to learning in a particular discipline, is now regarded as suspect.

It is difficult not to perceive the irony of this. University institutions should thrive on discussion and debate and disagreement within a subject; not any longer! People are being 'no-platformed' for simply declaring that men and women are biologically different; something which the Bible confirms right back to the time of Adam and Eve. It must be difficult for people who feel that they have been born into the wrong body (gender dysphoria), but the whole issue has got out of hand. People, such as teachers, are losing their jobs because they refuse to address students with what are now deemed to be the correct pronouns. What is really disturbing, however, is the rapidity with which gender dysphoria has become manifest in society, the meek way government has embraced it and the intolerance with which this is now being advanced by the transgender lobby. Teenage girls are being encouraged to take drugs and undergo irreversible operations to change their sex which they later publicly regret.[9]

Interestingly, it has created strife among women. The feminist movement who worked long and hard to achieve basic rights among women, find the transgender lobby a threat to what they have achieved. They are particularly concerned about safe spaces for women such as toilets, changing rooms and hospital wards.

The western nations, in particular the United States and the United Kingdom with their protestant traditions, are rapidly departing from the democratic norms they have been blessed with over many years. It does not take much spiritual discernment for Christians to see the hand of Satan behind much of this 'woke', anti-liberal agenda.

Part II of the book

In the next part of the book, we are going to examine the weapons for our warfare and how we can tackle Satan's attacks on God's commandments and the strongholds he has established in both individuals and society in general.

NOTES

1. Senator Edward Kennedy, the youngest sibling, did himself wonder whether the family was cursed. Google: *Ted Kennedy spoke of a family curse after Chappaquiddick. He had good reason.* (Washington Post 6th April 2018)

2. We have seen that in many pagan and idolatrous groups Satan hides his true identity under assumed names such as Baal, Jabulon, Sun god, Moon god, etc. People who worship in this way are more than likely to be aware that they are in contact with the spirit world, but they may not be aware that Satan himself is behind these false gods.

   However, Satan comes into the open in the practice of Satanism and witchcraft. From Satan's point of view this must be the most pleasing outcome. However, such direct worship is too brazen for many people and Satan is happy to remain hidden (the meaning of the word **occult**) in such circumstances. We should remember that Satan's principal objective is to deflect people from worshipping the one true God, and from accepting the salvation offered by God's Son, Jesus Christ.

   There are excellent books on the Christian ministry of healing and deliverance, some of which will be listed in the bibliography. There are also excellent ministries established to bring teaching, healing and deliverance from demonic power – *Ellel Ministries, Prayer Warriors International* and *Sozo International* to name just three.

3. A new book *"God, Help Me!"* – a true story by *Pastor Greg Hibbins* recounts his own experience of being a child medium in a spiritualist family in Rhodesia. Fortunately Jesus Christ reached down and touched him dramatically and he was led out of this life into a living faith in Christ, eventually becoming a pastor.

4. Pornography deserves a special mention because sadly it has become a problem for many Christian men and women and even pastors. *(I am assured on good authority that pornography is now a widespread problem for women as well as men.)* People may have taken to watching pornography because there are problems in their marriage. When they accept that it is wrong and want to escape from it, they find this enormously difficult. They may have been drawn into it through carnal desire or even through demonic

prompting, but long-term exposure to the visual images can cause a physiological change to their nervous systems. Reversing this requires real commitment starting with repentance before the Lord, and perhaps an agreement to meet regularly with a Christian mentor. (It is worth reading Chapter 4 on pornography in Emma Waring's book for Christian couples, *Seasons of Sex and Intimacy*.)

5. The acceptance by government and society of lifestyles different to the traditional heterosexual relationship has come upon Western society with such speed that many people cannot keep up with the terminology and acronyms. The principal acronym LGBT stands for Lesbian, Gay, Bisexual or Transgender. This however has been added to, so that we now have LGBT+ where the plus can include letters like A and Q. A in turn can mean ally (i.e. support of LGBT people) or Asexual. Q is a strange term because it means "Queer", a term that gay people used to consider a derogatory term for homosexual or lesbian, but has now been reclaimed by some homosexual people. The maelstrom of terms is confusing to say the least! A helpful glossary is found on the website: <www.parentinfo.org/article/gbtq-glossary-for-parents>. Readers should be aware that the article has been written for parents of children who have "come out' as gay or transgender and is supportive of these lifestyles.

6. Counselling: both Christian and secular is available for those women who are wondering whether to have or whether not to proceed with an abortion. Such counselling is also available for those women who have had abortions and who need to seek help afterwards. The world, for the most part, is not keen to recognise that many women suffer depression following abortion and may have great difficulty in recovering from it. Christian counsellors do recognise the inevitable problems associated with the unnatural practice of abortion.

7. Another area of conflict is whether to abort a foetus with birth defects or disabilities, which are now easily detected in the womb, in a way that was not possible in earlier times. All I would say to this is that most Christians take the view that their disabled child's life is precious in the sight of God and that they wish to honour this life. Both parents and children will testify to God's grace in such situations and the tremendous love they have felt for their disabled child. When interviewed, disabled adults are usually very aggrieved by the suggestion that their lives should have been terminated. They have accepted their handicaps but have lived life to the full within the parameters of their disability.

8. The word 'woke' has come into mainstream language in recent years. It has come to mean being aware of (or awake to) social injustice, in particular racial injustice and is very much associated with the 'Black lives matter' movement. This may sound a reasonable approach to such issues, but in practice it has led to intolerance and suppression of other people's views

9. One just has to Google 'young people regret sex changes' to find a variety of articles on this subject. There is rising concern among the medical profession at the rapid rise in applications to change one's sex among teenagers under the age of eighteen. The NHS was also told by the Government in February 2022 to close the Tavistock child gender identity clinic, after it was criticised in an independent review.

PART II

GOD'S ANSWER TO SATAN'S KINGDOM IS SPIRITUAL WARFARE

So far this book has been about what Satan has done to the human race. The second part is about how the Church can respond to this and take the warfare to the enemy

PART II

GOD'S ANSWER TO SATAN'S KINGDOM IS SPIRITUAL WARFARE

CHAPTER 8

SPIRITUAL WARFARE

In Part I of this book, I demonstrated how Satan has waged war against the commandments of God and his rules for living. In doing this, he has taken fallen humanity further into his kingdom of darkness. In Part II I intend to show how the Church can fight back and turn the tables on Satan. How the Church, through spiritual warfare, can help to release Satan's captives for salvation in God's kingdom. **In short, the Church no longer needs to remain a reluctant warrior; it can instead become a bold one.**

We have God's assurance that he wants to save people from Satan's kingdom and from hell.

God is not willing that any should perish, but that all should come to repentance.

(2 Peter 3:9 KJV)

God our Saviour, who wants all men to be saved and to come to a knowledge of the truth.

(1 Timothy 2:4 NIV)

What is the battleground?

We can see from these verses that the battleground is every unsaved human heart across the earth. The battle has been in two distinct parts. We have seen how the world was made captive to Satan through Adam's sin. We saw in Chapter 4 that this gave Satan a legal right to hold the human race captive, but Christ's victory on the Cross broke this legal right. Only Christ could do this, and the victory on the Cross of Calvary constituted the first part of the battle.

He [Jesus] disarmed the rulers and authorities and put them to open shame, by triumphing over them in it [the Cross].

(Colossians 2:15)

. . . . which he [God the Father] accomplished in Christ when he raised him from the dead and made him sit at his right hand in the heavenly places, far above all rule and authority and power and dominion, and above every name that is named, not only in this age, but also in that which is to come; and he has put all things under his feet and has made him the head over all things for the Church, which is his body, the fullness of him who fills all in all.

(Ephesians 1:20-23 RSV)

People now have the opportunity of salvation, but they are still held captive until they accept what Christ has done for them. Satan has fought a rear-guard action to blind humanity to what Christ has done. This way they remain captives and go into a lost eternity.

This brings us to the second part of the battle. This belongs to the Church under Christ's direction. He has given the Church the responsibility to assist the captives to realise their release from Satan's kingdom. **The captives need to hear the word of salvation, they need to see the power of God in action, and they need to be prayed for.**

Why is it a battle?

It is a battle because Satan resists God's attempt to reconcile humanity to himself; Satan wishes to keep the human race captive and to take people to hell, a place made for him and his fallen angels (*Matthew 25:41*) and not for the human race. Many Christians believe that all that is needed is for people to hear the message of salvation. Following this each person then makes the choice to accept salvation or reject it. Would that it were so simple!

The parable of the sower spreading his seed on different types of soil helps us here (*Matthew 13:3-9, 18-23*). The message of salvation is the seed. Some people have open hearts and yearn for God. Here the seed falls on fertile soil. Others welcome the seed, but it does not take root and where difficulties or persecutions arise, they fall away. Others are directly attacked by Satan's kingdom. Demonic forces snatch away the message, so it falls on stony ground, or they crowd it out with weeds that stifle and confuse the message. People in these last two categories may be strongly captive to Satan; they may be captive to ancestral iniquity or family curses. Either way Satan is able to blind them to the truth. **We see from this parable that merely hearing the word does not necessarily open the door to salvation.** If Satan and his kingdom had been bound from holding the human race captive following Christ's death and resurrection, then salvation would only involve hearing the Gospel. People would have a simple choice: they would either accept the free gift of salvation or reject it, preferring spiritual darkness to light (*John 3:19*).

However, Satan has not been bound in this way. God in his wisdom has decided to involve the Church in the process of bringing people to repentance and salvation. It is this that constitutes the second part or stage of the battle.

The manifold wisdom of God

> *. . . . and to make all men see what is the plan of the mystery hidden for ages in God who created all things; that through the Church the **manifold wisdom of God** might now be made known to the principalities and powers in the heavenly places.*
> *(Ephesians 3:9-10 RSV)* [emphasis added]

> *[God] . . . . made us alive together with Christ (by grace you have been saved) and raised us up with him **and made us sit with him in the heavenly places** in Christ Jesus.*
> *(Ephesians 2:5-6 RSV)* [emphasis added]

This second verse tells us that the Church occupies an exalted position. It is seated in the heavenly places from where it wages spiritual warfare. This is why it is so important to pray in the Spirit as the apostle Paul urges (*Ephesians 6:18*) in order to ensure that we are indeed seated in these heavenly places.

The Church is used to dislodge this satanic occupying force and to set the captives free. It is a **brilliant strategy** because it uses the captives already freed, to fight on behalf of those still waiting to be set free. God's manifold wisdom (*Ephesians 3:10*) is being displayed to the discomfort of Satan's rulers and authorities in the heavenly places. No wonder Satan is angry and resists such activity by the Church. Unfortunately, he has been very effective in deflecting the Church from this important role throughout its history.

The completeness of Christ's victory over Satan, sin and death

Before we take a look at the Church's role in spiritual warfare, it is a good idea to be clear on just what Christ achieved in his victory over Satan. We saw earlier in the chapter, the power vested in Christ following his victory on the Cross (*Ephesians 1:20-23*). Let us note some other verses which emphasise the completeness of Christ's victory over Satan:

> *He has delivered us from the dominion of darkness and transferred us to the kingdom of his beloved Son.*
>
> *(Colossians 1:13 RSV)*

> *That you may declare the wonderful deeds of him who called you out of darkness into his marvellous light.*
>
> *(1 Peter 2:9 RSV)*

> *Have this mind among yourselves, which is yours in Christ Jesus, who though he was in the form of God, did not count equality with God a thing to be grasped, but made himself nothing, taking the form of a servant, being born in the likeness of men. And being found in human form, he humbled himself by becoming obedient to the point of death, even death on a cross. **Therefore God has highly exalted him** and bestowed on him the name that is above every name, so that at the name of Jesus every knee should bow, in heaven and on earth and under the earth, and every tongue confess that Jesus Christ is Lord, to the glory of God the Father.*
>
> *(Philippians 2:5-11)* [emphasis added]

> *Since therefore the children share in flesh and blood, he [Jesus] himself likewise partook of the same nature, that through death he might destroy him who has the power of death, that is, the devil, and deliver all those who through fear of death were subject to lifelong bondage.*
>
> *(Hebrews 2:14-15 RSV)*

> *Now in putting everything in subjection to him [Jesus], he left nothing outside his control. At present, we do not yet see everything in subjection to him.*
>
> *(Hebrews 2:8)*

In these verses we see the power of Christ's victory on the Cross. The last verse however brings us to the part to be enacted by the Church. The devil is still at large, despite his monumental defeat by Christ, but God in his wisdom wants us, the Church, to assist him in bringing many souls to Christ and rolling back the kingdom of darkness. If one thinks about it, God could have removed each one of us from earth to heaven the moment we were saved, but he has not done this. Instead, he has chosen to leave us here for our natural lifespan, in order to help bring many human captives to salvation. **This means engaging in spiritual warfare, not just as individuals, but also as the Church. We are to be co-workers with God in the establishment of his kingdom in human hearts.**

The Church as an army

As we begin to look at this idea of the Church as an army, I want to say that there are many excellent books on spiritual warfare, either for individual ministry or more widely for the Church[1&2]. Nevertheless, one can be left wondering exactly how believers or the Church are expected to wage this warfare. My intention is to make this book practical. It is both theological in defining the issues, but also practical in how to engage the enemy. I highlight the preparation needed and the tools available, **but my practical suggestions are not meant to be a template for action.** I present ideas as to how this warfare may be waged. If church leaders agree with my thesis that this warfare is necessary and they wish to act on it, then they must decide what is appropriate for their situation. Most of us understand that God does not like to be tied down and that he may lead the readers to rather different strategies of warfare than those I suggest.

However, it will be a major achievement if leaders accept the challenge that the Church at large and their churches in particular, need to engage in spiritual warfare. If the Lord leads them to different methods from those I suggest, then that is fine. Human armies do not conform to a blueprint, and they too have different ways of waging war.

What we can all agree on, however, is that this warfare will only succeed if it originates with the Lord (our Captain-General) and he leads it.

NOTES

1. Some of these books are listed in the Bibliography and marked with an asterisk. Any Christian seeking individual prayer and ministry should first approach their church pastor or elders. These leaders may then offer the Church's prayer and help or they may agree to refer them to an outside organisation that has particular experience of healing and deliverance.

2. David Tidy's book 'Discerning the Mixture' is interesting because it touches on the territorial aspects of Satan's kingdom and the importance of unearthing the history of where buildings such as churches are built – a whole subject in itself!

CHAPTER 9

INTERCESSORS

Before we discuss the Church's activity in spiritual warfare, I wish to say something about intercessors. **Intercession** is a special kind of prayer where God calls individuals or a group of people to become immersed in prayer and spiritual warfare in a way unknown to most Christians. The person or group come fully into harmony with the Holy Spirit and he directs their prayers. However, there is a further stage where the Spirit not only directs the prayers, but he puts a spiritual burden on the person so that they truly identify with the situation or people they are praying for. This is no light matter for two reasons: first, the person may fully identify with the pain and the sin in the situation for which they are called to intercede. Secondly, they may have to wrestle in prayer for a long time before the breakthrough comes and they know that the prayer has been answered. Sometimes they may have to take a break from prayer while still carrying the burden and then return to it later[1].

The scriptural basis for intercession

In the New Testament the scriptural basis for intercession is revealed in *Romans 8:18-27*. Its enactment in the life of the apostle Paul is revealed in *Romans 9* and *10*. In *Romans 9:2-4* Paul utters the astonishing words concerning his kinsmen the Israelites:

> *For I could wish that I myself were accursed and cut off from Christ for the sake of my brothers, my kinsmen according to the flesh.*

Here he is identifying with the Jews who face a lost eternity and whom Paul wishes to see saved (*Romans 10:1*). As he does so he experiences great anguish. He testifies that the Jews have all the blessings inherited from the patriarchs, but not the knowledge of what Christ has done for them.

The Old Testament is full of examples of intercession by the great men of faith such as Moses and Daniel. We cannot know how Moses felt as he interceded, but we can see him flat on his face or standing between the Israelites and God's intended judgement. On two occasions he caused God to relent from his intention to destroy the Israelites for their sin and rebellion (*Exodus 32; Numbers 14*).

Daniel was a great man of faith and prayer. In *Daniel 9* we find him praying that God will enact the prophecy given to Jeremiah which said that after 70 years the Jews would return from exile to Jerusalem and their land. Daniel understood that the prophecy would not just happen, but that God had called him to pray it into being. Daniel fasted and was mourning during the time of prayer. He confessed his own sins and those of Israel. He thus identified with the sins of Israel even though he himself was a very godly man. Like Moses, Daniel was a very humble man.

It is worth mentioning other means of identification with the sins of Israel found in the Old Testament. Sometimes God required a prophet to enact something that revealed the sins of the people. Hosea was required to marry a prostitute, to reveal that God considered that the Israelites had prostituted themselves with pagan gods.

Ezekiel was given the thankless task of lying on his side bound with ropes for 390 days and then on his other side for 40 days in order to identify first with the sins of Israel and then with the sins of Judah (*Ezekiel 4*).

Today we might not consider these enactments to be intercessory, but they certainly identified with Israel's sin and they were most definitely sacrificial.

Intercessors will be well versed in scripture and the Holy Spirit may lead them to use scriptures in a way that most of us might not anticipate. The Psalms and Proverbs are a wonderful resource for verses that can be claimed or proclaimed to bring victory in a given situation.

The cost of intercession

This kind of prayer can be spiritually, mentally and physically exhausting. In extreme cases it may even shorten a prayer warrior's life. A famous intercessor in Britain was the Welshman Rees Howells who founded a Bible College in Wales. Previously Rees and his wife had been missionaries in Africa, but God called him to found the college in the 1920s at the same time calling him to a life of intercession. The Lord called Rees, the college staff and students to intercede at crucial times during World War II. Reading the accounts of his life there can be no doubt that he and his fellow intercessors were instrumental in defeating Hitler[2]. Satan had raised up Hitler to dominate the world and at the same time to destroy the Jewish people through the Holocaust.

Rees died at the age of 70, a few years after the war. His son Samuel took over as director of the Bible College. Samuel described movingly how he would slip into his father's room during the war to find Rees slumped and exhausted, as pale as death and bathed in perspiration. Such was the agony he was experiencing as he carried the intercession. It eventually broke him physically. Up until then he had been a strong person, with incredible stamina[3]. Nevertheless, this burden continued after the war as Rees Howells continued to intercede, this time for the establishment of a nation for the Jews which happened through 1947 and 1948.

Secret intercessors

The burden carried by Rees Howells was exceptional both in its pressure and in its duration. Most intercession will not be as severe as this. However, there are intercessors all over the world, many known only to God, who are carrying burdens placed in their hearts by the Holy Spirit. They are actually feeling the pain, anger and compassion which God feels as he looks down on his fallen world. They are wrestling against the satanic forces contributing to the sin and wickedness that causes such pain in God's heart.

Other prayer warriors

Besides intercessors there are many praying people who do understand about Satan's kingdom and who pray faithfully, either individually or in groups, to further God's purposes here on earth. Like the intercessors, such prayer warriors will constitute a minority of Christians worldwide.

My question is this. Surely God would want much more of his large worldwide Church to be involved in prayer and intercession than is currently the case? I am confident that we are now in the end-times before Christ's return to earth[4]. Surely God will want his Church to rise up in prayer and intercession as we approach the dark days of the Tribulation prior to the Lord's return? Jesus said:

> We must work the works of him who sent me while it is day; night is coming when no one can work. As long as I am in the world, I am the light of the world.
>
> (John 9:4-5)

Given the last sentence, it is clear that this refers to spiritual light and dark and that a time is coming when spreading the gospel in the face of satanic opposition will become extremely difficult.

The spectrum of belief concerning the devil

There is a whole spectrum of believers in their approach to Satan and his kingdom of darkness. A quick survey reveals five categories of Christians. They range from:

1. Christians who think that it is incorrect to personify evil as the devil. Satan is a name for evil in the world, not a living spiritual entity. Demonic behaviour is not due to spirit beings. It is an illness or an unwelcome condition.

2. Christians who recognise that Satan is a spiritual being and that he helps to drive evil in the world through tempting people. Apart from resisting the temptation, he is to be left well alone. They may not appreciate that he oversees a kingdom of fallen angels and demonic spirits.

3. Christians who do understand the existence of Satan, his kingdom and his opposition to God's work of salvation. However, through lack of teaching, they do not know whether to pray about it or how they should pray.

4. Christians who do believe it is right to challenge the devil's activities and want to do so. However, they may not be organised to do it and they may run into trouble as they try to tackle Satan on their own.

5. Finally, there are the prayer warriors and the intercessors who have been led into spiritual warfare. They have been trained by the Holy Spirit to know God's heart and to take on the enemy when called to do so.

I have bracketed the prayer warriors and the intercessors together because they both understand the satanic kingdom and they both engage with it. They understand the need to be led by the Holy Spirit and when to pray alone or with other believers. However, the intercessor carries God's burden in a way that the prayer warrior does not. This author has wept and got angry in the Spirit as he has prayed for people or situations, but he has never carried God's burden in the way described earlier in this chapter.

I believe that intercessors can only be chosen by God. He does this for particular tasks. When much of the Church is asleep to the activities of Satan and his kingdom, he may well rely on intercessors to achieve his purposes. However, I see no reason why the rest of us cannot volunteer to be **prayer warriors** whatever our starting point, be it categories 1, 2, 3 or 4 above. Once we are taught and understand about Satan and his kingdom then the role is open to us.

My thesis is that God wants much more of the Church to become involved and **to become part of a disciplined army** that will contribute to an end-time harvest of souls for the kingdom, an event prophesied over the years by a number of Christian leaders and prophets.

Conclusion

The rest of the book seeks to explore how this might come about. It compares the Church to a natural human army. This approach is new, and some Christian leaders may disagree with it. Nevertheless, I would ask them to keep an open mind until they have read the rest of the book.

NOTES

1. Not surprisingly many intercessor groups operate in a hidden way. They are called by the Lord and their relationship to the Lord is very personal. One group I am familiar with is **Dovetail Shalom Ministries** who have more of a public profile than many groups. Their emphasis is intercession for Israel and for the United Kingdom.

2. This statement is in no way meant to diminish the contribution of many other Christians who prayed for Hitler's defeat. In fact, King George VI called the nation to prayer on seven occasions during the war.

3. See *Samuel Rees Howells – a life of intercession* by *Richard Maton* Chapter 11, P.49.

4. See my book *The Return of Jesus Christ* (details in the Bibliography)

CHAPTER 10
THE CHURCH AS AN ARMY

The Church is a many-faceted body of millions of individuals, many now in heaven with the Lord and many still on earth. In the New Testament Jesus and the apostles Paul and Peter used metaphors to describe the various roles of the Church. There are seven of them which can be grouped as follows:

Salvation and the New Birth:
1.   The Shepherd and the sheep
2.   The last Adam and the new creation

Personal growth and the work of the Church on earth:
3.   The Vine and the branches
4.   The Head and the many-membered body

Temple worship and ministry to God:
5.   The Cornerstone and the stones of the building
6.   The High Priest and the kingdom of priests

The future:
7.   The Bridegroom and the Bride

There is one role that the Lord did not spell out in this way, but which can be discerned from many scriptures. **The Church (still on earth) is an army with Christ as its Captain-General**. The imprint of this role is found across the whole New Testament. Just as we see God as the Lord of Hosts in the Old Testament fighting the cause of Israel, so we see Christ in the New Testament fighting the cause of the kingdom of God. One of the problems for believers is that the emphasis throughout the Church age has been on Christ as Saviour and not on Christ as both Saviour and warrior. We have only to read John's description of the risen Christ at the beginning of the book of Revelation, to see a very different person from the Jesus who walked this earth in the gospels.

A Victorious Army

Let us look at what constitutes a victorious military army and then see how the text of the New Testament matches up to it. We can discern the following features in such an army:

1. A cause which the soldiers can share and believe
2. A leader whom the soldiers can trust
3. A chain of command which the soldiers understand
4. Armour and weaponry which is up to date and effective
5. Leaders and soldiers who know and understand their enemy
6. Soldiers who are trained, fit and disciplined
7. A united and obedient army – one that plans, works and fights together
8. An effective battle plan at various levels of operation
9. An army adept at defence as well as attack

I have devoted *Appendix 6* to examine how well the Church, at least in the western world, matches up to the characteristics of a victorious human army. Meanwhile, however, we will take a look at scriptures relevant to soldiers and warfare, from both the Old and New Testaments.

Scriptural references to soldiers and warfare

Let us start with two scriptures about the Commander, one from the New Testament and one from the Old.

Then I turned to see the voice that was speaking to me, and on turning I saw seven golden lampstands, and in the midst of the lampstands one like a Son of man, clothed with a long robe and with a golden sash round his chest. The hairs of his head were white, like white wool, like snow. His eyes were like a flame of fire, his feet were like burnished bronze, refined in a furnace, and his voice was like the roar of many waters. In his right hand he held seven stars, from his mouth came a sharp two-edged sword, and his face was like the sun shining in full strength.
(Revelation 1:12-16)

When Joshua was by Jericho, he lifted up his eyes and looked, and behold, a man was standing before him with his sword drawn in his hand. And Joshua went to him and said to him, "Are you for us, or for our adversaries?" and he said, "No, but I am the Commander of the army of the Lord. Now I have come." And Joshua fell on his face on the earth and worshipped and said to him, "What does my Lord say to his servant?" and the Commander of the Lord's army said to Joshua, "Take off your sandals from your feet, for the place where you are standing is holy." And Joshua did so.

(Joshua 5:13-15)

We do not have to analyse these passages to see that they are talking about two formidable figures with all the attributes of a warrior-leader. The New Testament passage is specifically referring to Christ and many theologians consider that the second passage is also referring to Christ in his pre-incarnate form.

The army to which the Joshua passage refers is the army of archangels and angels in the heavenly realms. We repeatedly find that this army works in parallel to the armies on the ground. In the Old Testament this was the physical army of Israel, while in the New Testament it is the praying army of saints in the Church.

The following verses reinforce the fact that the God of the Old Testament is a God of war. It is for this reason that he is often referred to as the Lord of hosts.

The Lord is a man of war, the Lord is his name.

(Exodus 15:3)

Who is this King of glory? The Lord, strong and mighty, mighty in battle.

(Psalm 24:8)

The Lord of hosts is mustering a host for battle.

(Isaiah 13:4)

References to soldiers and battle in the New Testament

We find the following references to soldiers, weapons and battle in the New Testament.

Share in suffering as a good soldier of Christ Jesus. No soldier gets entangled in civilian pursuits, since his aim is to please the one who enlisted him.

(Paul writing to Timothy: 2 Timothy 2:3-4)

For though we walk in the flesh, we are not waging war according to the flesh. For the weapons of our warfare are not of the flesh, but have divine power to destroy strongholds.

(2 Corinthians 10:3-4)

Finally, be strong in the Lord and in the strength of his might. Put on the whole armour of God, that you may be able to stand against the wiles of the devil. For we wrestle not against flesh and blood, but against principalities, against powers, against the rulers of the darkness of this world, against spiritual wickedness in high places [the heavenly places].

(Ephesians 6:10-12 KJV)

Fight the good fight of faith.

(1 Timothy 6:12)

This charge I entrust to you, Timothy, my child, in accordance with the prophecies previously made about you, that by them you may wage the good warfare.

(1 Timothy 1:18)

I have thought it necessary to send to you Epaphroditus my brother and fellow worker and fellow soldier. . . .

(Philippians 2:25)

Let us cast off the works of darkness and put on the armour of light.

(Romans 13:12)

When we reach Revelation, the last book of the New Testament, we find we are back to real physical wars, as we await the physical return of the Lord Jesus to earth. This is a time of unprecedented spiritual darkness when Satan is allowed to dominate the world through his human agent, the Antichrist, and where the futility of his rebellion against God is laid bare.

This is a time of both actual and spiritual warfare. The Antichrist wreaks terrible destruction on the world, the saints and on Israel. It is also a time of great witness of the Gospel to the world, especially by the 144,000 witnesses of *Revelation 7* and *Revelation 14*. The testimony of the saints is summed up in the verse:

> *They have conquered him [the devil] by the blood of the Lamb and by the word of their testimony, for they loved not their lives even unto death.*
>
> *(Revelation 12:11)*

This succinct verse indicates that the saints have prevailed against the devil, but often at the cost of their own earthly lives. Rather appropriately, it is the last book of the New Testament which reminds us that the Church is an army which is at war with our enemy, the devil.

God's weapons of warfare

It is now appropriate to examine the weapons of warfare available to God's soldiers. We will not restrict this to the New Testament. It is instructive to see how God wages warfare in the Old Testament through his chosen people Israel. This had both a physical and a spiritual aspect to the conflict.

In Old Testament times God's people, the Jews, had to fight their human foes in the flesh. They had to have an army and to engage in physical combat with the risk that they might die or suffer injury. Several times God is described as the Lord of hosts, and he is seen to be a military commander in charge of both angelic hosts and the Jewish human army on the ground. The Jewish people were often called to defeat their enemies in battle in the physical realm; King David was the prime example of a victorious military commander. Although this was physical warfare, God often intervened in the Old Testament to instruct the Israelites to do something other than physical fighting.

God chose to reveal himself through the valour of Israel in battle, but he also directed them to rely on his intervention. This may well have been to prevent Israel from becoming too self-reliant.

To give a few examples we have:

1. Israel succeeding in battle when Moses kept his hands raised (*Exodus 17:10-13*)

2. The fall of Jericho when the Israelites had to blow the shofar and march round the city for seven days (*Joshua 6*)

3. Israel is defeated in battle at Ai because of the sin of Achan (*Joshua 7*).

4. David seeks God as to whether he should attack the Philistines. In one instance God tells him to attack and in the following instance God tells him to wait, until he hears the sound of marching in the balsam trees (*1 Chronicles 14*).

5. Several times in the Old Testament God causes Israel's enemies to fight among and thus destroy themselves. We see this between King Saul and the Philistines (*1 Samuel 14:15-23*) and again when Jehoshaphat is threatened by the Moabites and Ammonites (*2 Chronicles 20*). The significant thing about this battle is that Jehoshaphat first sought the guidance of the Lord in front of all the people in Jerusalem. The Lord then called a prophet to respond, during which he said: *"Do not be afraid or discouraged because of this vast army. **For the battle is not yours, but God's.**"* (2 Chronicles 20:15)

6. On a later occasion in the Old Testament God sent an angel of destruction to destroy a whole army. This was the occasion when Sennacherib, the king of Assyria, besieged King Hezekiah in Jerusalem. Just like Jehoshaphat before him, Hezekiah sought the Lord, and God sent the prophet Isaiah to inform him that Sennacherib would not attack and the siege of Jerusalem would be lifted (*2 Kings 19*).

We thus see in the Old Testament a combination of physical warfare and God's supernatural deliverance. Despite the obvious physical nature of the warfare in the Old Testament, there is an interesting revelation of the parallel warfare occurring in the heavenly realms between God's angels and the forces of Satan. Elisha's servant is afraid of the forces of the King of Aram who surround and threaten them. Elisha tells him not to be afraid and then asks the Lord to open his spiritual eyes. When the Lord does this the servant sees mountains full of horses and chariots of fire all around Elisha (*2 Kings 6:8-23*). **For every battle there is an angelic army parallel to what is happening on earth.**

The brutality of Old Testament warfare

Christians often wonder why the warfare of the Old Testament had to be so brutal. This is not an easy question to answer. The matter goes right back to the early chapters of Genesis. Following Satan's success in persuading Eve and then Adam to sin, God gave three judgements. The first was to the serpent who embodied Satan:

> *I will put enmity between you and the woman, and between your offspring and her offspring; he shall bruise your head, and you shall bruise his heel.*
>
> *(Genesis 3:15)*

Bible scholars are confident that the reference to offspring (*or seed*) refers not only to the generations that followed Adam and Eve, but also to one particular male descendant. This was to be the coming Messiah (Christ) who through his crucifixion inflicted a fatal wound to the head of Satan.

Since that time Satan has sought to destroy this seed at every opportunity and God in turn has sought to protect the woman's seed. Satan's first effort was to contaminate the human race through the union of fallen angelic beings with human women (*Genesis 6*). This is one reason why God chose to destroy the human race in Noah's day. The race was becoming contaminated by the Nephilim (giants); the illicit offspring of satanic angels with women.

The seed was narrowed down to a chosen people when God created the Israelite (*Hebrew*) race through Abraham, Isaac and Jacob. Satan then adopted a two-pronged attack. At times in history, he sought to destroy the Jewish people (see *the Book of Esther*) and at other times he sought to contaminate the race through interbreeding with the surrounding pagan tribes. The Israelites were particularly vulnerable as they were entering the Promised Land where they were told to drive out or kill their pagan neighbours. During its subsequent history the surrounding nations frequently attacked Israel and were vanquished or driven off by Israel's armies under God's guiding hand. We thus see that Israel's survival was a matter of life and death and often required a decisive response; something that should not be lost on Israel's enemies today!

I think we can see that God's harsh treatment of Israel's enemies in the Old Testament arose first from his abhorrence at their evil pagan practices and secondly from his desire to see that Israel did not become contaminated by such practices.

Despite this, Satan had considerable success in deflecting Israel from God's purposes, by causing them to intermarry with neighbouring tribes and to worship pagan idols. By the time of the two kingdoms, Israel and Judah, this problem of contamination became increasingly serious, and God acted on the warnings he had given to Moses (see *Deuteronomy 28*). He sent, first Israel and then 100 years later Judah, into exile in foreign lands[1].

However, Satan was never going to prevent the arrival of God's chosen Messiah and Saviour, Jesus Christ, who arrived on time to open the door to salvation for both Jews and Gentiles.

Satan has continued to harass the Jews throughout history, both out of hatred and also to try to prevent the return of Jesus Christ and thus prevent Satan's own demise. Protection of God's seed from the first woman, Eve, has been an on-going theme from the start of the Bible.

New Testament Warfare

In the New Testament everything changes. Believers in Jesus are born again in their spirits and they have a direct relationship with Jesus and the Father through the Holy Spirit.

The warfare with Satan is just as strong as it has ever been. Satan now seeks to prevent people coming to salvation through Christ, but the battle has changed for three reasons:

1. Christ has won the victory over Satan on the Cross (*Colossians 2:15*). This enables human beings to have a personal spiritual relationship with God the Father, Jesus the Son and the Holy Spirit.

2. Jesus has removed Satan's legal right to hold the human race captive (See Chapter 4). Individuals can now be reconciled to God if they so wish. In *Revelation 1:18* the risen Christ says to John the apostle: *"I have the keys of death and Hades* (hell)." These keys have thus been taken away from Satan and his angels.

3. The conflict is now carried out in the spiritual realm. This means the weapons of warfare and the spiritual battle change from Old Testament times.

The physical weapons of Old Testament times such as swords, spears, arrows and shields are replaced by spiritual weapons.[2] I will list the weapons available in the next chapter and then discuss whether they are defensive, offensive or both.

Let us first remind ourselves that the objective of the warfare is **to extend the kingdom of God on earth by bringing human souls to salvation through Jesus.** Preaching the biblical message of salvation is therefore very important, but preaching alone is not necessarily sufficient to bring people to salvation. People may need to be set free from demonic bondages and ancestral or other curses. They may need to see the power of God to deliver and heal. They may simply need to be prayed for by concerned family and and friends.

Conclusion

Every believer needs to recognise that once we become Christians we are at war with Satan's kingdom of darkness. If Satan succeeds in blinding us to this fact and causes us to become passive Christians, thankful that we are saved for eternity but not obligated to work for the kingdom, then he may well leave us alone. If, however, we recognise the call to work for the kingdom in whatever way God calls us, then we may become very aware of his opposition. We may learn to use the weapons of defence, but still be unaware that God actually wants to go on the offensive against this arch foe. The next chapter will reveal the extensive range of weapons available to the Church as an army.

NOTES

1. See my book: *Has God really finished with Israel?* (details in the Bibliography)

2. We should remember that while Christians are involved in spiritual warfare, human wars still continue on earth. In fact, the twentieth century saw World Wars I and II, the greatest conflicts in human history. Christians like other citizens may be called to fight and die in such wars on behalf of their country. This, however, is separate from their calling to engage in spiritual warfare.

   These physical wars are stirred up and energised by Satan and his angelic princes ruling over a nation (such as the Prince of Persia, seen in the book of Daniel). Spiritual warfare is very much needed in such situations. God caused intercessors like Rees Howells to wage incessant spiritual warfare during World War II to ensure that the evil of Nazism was defeated. In those more religious days, the King called the people of Britain to pray, and the people responded at seven critical junctures during the war.

CHAPTER 11
GOD'S WEAPONS OF WARFARE

It is a good exercise to list and then examine the weapons available to the Church as an army. Many Christians are not aware of all that is available to them in this way. Nevertheless, we need to bear in mind the Old Testament scripture:

Unless the Lord builds the house, those who build it labour in vain.

(Psalm 127:1)

In waging war against our enemy we are building the Lord's house by bringing people to salvation in Christ. The Lord wants us to use these weapons, but always under his direction.

1. The armour of God
2. The baptism in the Holy Spirit
3. Praise and worship to God
4. Confession of sin and forgiveness
5. Proclamation of scripture – God's living Word
6. Waiting on the Lord
7. Prayer:

    Prayer and fasting

    Intercessory prayer

    Praying in 'tongues'

    The blood of Jesus

    Prayer walking – claiming ground
8. Binding & Loosing (binding the strongman)
9. Evangelism – speaking to people about salvation
10. Deliverance & Healing

11. Post-conversion care

12. Covering

The Church is most definitely equipped with armour and weaponry, both defensive and offensive, which is fully up to date in the warfare with Satan. Let us examine this armour.

Author's note: This is a long chapter and readers may prefer to come back to it after they have read the rest of the book to see how I develop the theme of the Church as an army.

1. The armour of God (Ephesians 6)

This is mostly defensive and assists in protecting us during spiritual warfare. The apostle Paul tells us to put on the helmet of **Salvation**, the breastplate of **Righteousness**, the belt of **Truth** and the shoes of the **Gospel of Peace**. We should take the shield of **Faith** in one hand and the sword of the Spirit which is the **Word of God** in the other hand.

Paul says **put on** the armour of God and I think that is exactly what we should do each day. I used to think that it was in position as a matter of course, but my wife and I now **declare** that we are putting on the armour each day.[1] Remember too, that it is only effective if we fulfil the qualities listed. If we are knowingly unrighteous or untruthful then the armour will not help us. All this armour is defensive, but the Word of God has the added quality of being offensive which is why is it called a sword.

2. The Baptism in the Holy Spirit

Jesus prepared his disciples for his departure by telling them that he would send them another Counsellor/Comforter, the Holy Spirit who would dwell in them (*John 14, 15* and *Acts 1*). In *Acts 2* the disciples discovered what this meant while they waited in prayer on the day of Pentecost. The Spirit empowered them to preach the gospel and to exercise the nine gifts of the Holy Spirit. These gifts and their purpose are described in detail by Paul in *1 Corinthians 12-14*. The The New Testament is full of the exploits of the apostles and disciples working under the power of the Holy Spirit.

Sadly some in the Church today still deny the experience of this baptism in the Holy Spirit, but countless numbers of Christians can testify to its power in their lives and in their ability to witness to the gospel. Paul warns that the gifts must be exercised in the context of an ordered and disciplined church. Christians baptised in this way are operating in a supernatural realm and can be very aware of the activities of Satan. The baptism is a kind of overarching military covering providing for both defensive and offensive warfare.[2]

3. Praise and worship

Praising and giving glory to God can be a very powerful weapon, both defensive and offensive. Praise brings the presence of God into the midst of us and sends the enemy fleeing; he cannot stand the glory of God. It is therefore a good idea to start every prayer meeting with worship and praise.

I remember an occasion quite early in my Christian life when my wife and I had been counselling a young woman and had persuaded her to keep her baby and then release it for adoption, rather than have an abortion. We were driving home in the dark from a function when I noticed a car harassing us by driving right up behind us. It was very unnerving and went on for some time. So I said, *"Let's praise the Lord at the top of our voices!"* We did this and within moments the car overtook us and sped away. I connected the spiritual battle we had had in the previous weeks before the young woman decided to go full term, to the harassment by the young men in the car. I like to think that something about our praise (which of course they could not hear) spooked them and sent them speeding away!

4. Confession of sin and forgiveness

Few people realise what powerful weapons these are.

Confession of sin

Confession of sin is essential when we first come to Christ to accept his offer of salvation. We confess our sins, say sorry to God and thank him for our salvation in Jesus. By repenting, we declare that we are turning from our former sinful life. We may also need to repent at later times in our Christian life if we have knowingly sinned or turned our backs on God.

What many Christians do not know is that it is possible and right to confess on behalf of other people when we are interceding for the nation. Some Christians are puzzled by this, believing it is right to confess their own sin but not to confess it for anyone else. Nevertheless, there are several occasions in the Old Testament when God calls upon his people, the Jews, to do exactly this [3].

> But if they confess their iniquity and **the iniquity of their fathers** in the treachery that they committed against me . . . then I will remember my covenant with Jacob . . . and I will remember the land.
> *(Leviticus 26:40, 42)* [emphasis added]

> And the Israelites separated themselves from all foreigners and stood and confessed their sins and **the iniquities of their fathers**.
> *(Nehemiah 9:2)* [emphasis added]

> While I was speaking and praying, confessing my sin **and the sin of my people Israel** and presenting my plea before the Lord my God for the holy hill of my God . . .
> *(Daniel 9:20)* [emphasis added]

(It is worth reading *Daniel 9:3-19* to follow the content of Daniel's confession)

Confession of sin on behalf of our ancestors makes perfect sense when we remember that when God gave the Ten Commandments (*Exodus 20*) to Moses he made it clear that for the very serious sin of idolatry, he would visit the iniquity of the fathers on the children to the third and fourth generation.

Like Daniel, modern-day intercessors may feel led to confess on behalf of their nation when they are asking God to intervene for the nation. This kind of prayer can have dramatic results[4]. What it does is to help weaken or even break the hold that Satan has over a family, city or nation. Sin, especially the sin of idolatry, allows Satan access to control people, families, cities and nations. Christians can confess the sins of their ancestors, city or nation which had led to this control.

Consequently confession is a powerful weapon in spiritual warfare.

Forgiveness

This is not so much a weapon as a necessary act of defence. Forgiveness is an essential act for Christians. The Bible is crystal clear about this. We must not hold onto wrongs that have been done to us. Jesus said:

> *For if you forgive others their trespasses, your heavenly Father will also forgive you, but if you do not forgive others their trespasses, neither will your Father forgive your trespasses.*
> *(Matthew 6:14-15)*

It is helpful to remember that forgiveness is an act of the will, it is not a feeling. This usually comes later.

5. Proclamation - Speaking out the Word of God

Derek Prince, one of the great Christian teachers of the twentieth century, believed this to be a very powerful weapon and it can be used both defensively and offensively. We do this at one of the prayer groups I lead. We usually stand and then speak the words of a biblical passage into the heavenly realms. We consciously speak the words to the enemy. Alternatively we might remind the Lord of his word on a particular subject.

In a defensive situation we might say for example:

> *No weapon formed against me (us) will prevail and I (we) shall refute every tongue that accuses me (us).*
> *(Isaiah 54:17)*

In an offensive situation we might declare:

> *The weapons we fight with have divine power to demolish strongholds. We demolish arguments and every pretension that sets itself up against the knowledge of God . . . . . [followed by the name of the stronghold we wish to demolish]*
> *(2 Corinthians 10:4-5)*

If we are praying for a particular thing to happen such as the Jews returning to Israel, then we might proclaim some of the many verses declaring that God will do this. God does not, of course, need reminding, but we do believe that he likes us to quote scripture back to him.

6. Waiting on the Lord

This is not a weapon as such, but it is very much part of warfare strategy and tactics. **It is actually the most important part of the meeting!** As we shall see in the next chapter, there is one very big difference between a human army and the Lord's army. In the Lord's army each unit, however small, can hear directly from the Commander in Chief. He will have a strategy for every battle at whatever level. When we have spent time praising and worshiping the Lord, putting on the armour, reviewing the situation as we see it, we need to ask the Holy Spirit to direct the meeting and then wait to hear from him. This is where we shall learn the strategy and tactics for this particular battle. He may surprise us!

7. Prayer

Most Christians do not think in terms of warfare, but if they did, then prayer would be the one weapon that came to mind. Prayer is indeed ubiquitous to the Church – any believer can and should participate in it. Prayer is both defensive and offensive. Most regular prayer is probably defensive: it centres on asking God to do something for us such as blessing, protection, healing or provision. It becomes an offensive weapon however, when we pray for someone to be saved: relatives, friends and work colleagues and indeed the nation's leaders. Paul tells us to pray for those in authority over us (*1 Timothy 2:1-4*).

John, the writer of Revelation, describes golden bowls full of incense, which are the prayers of the saints (*Revelation 5:8*). The implication is that prayers can be stored up by God until they reach a tipping point and he is ready to act. This is one explanation for why prayers may not be answered immediately – it most certainly does not mean they are wasted.

Satan most definitely does not like us to pray for people. I remember a time in my life when a lot of people came across my path blaspheming the name of Jesus, and regrettably I was not standing up for him. Eventually I realised that God was giving me an opportunity to challenge this blasphemy and so I started to respond by saying that I knew Jesus as my Saviour. Usually it elicited a blank response; sometimes an apology and sometimes anger. What I said did not really matter, but I resolved to pray for every such person's salvation. It was amazing how quickly the blasphemy stopped! I still try to do this but am sensitive to the situation. It may not be wise to say this when alone, to a drunk person in a dark street!

Many Christians are not aware that Satan takes prayer seriously. He has his own prayer warriors among people who are into the deep things of Satan (*Revelation 2:24*). These would include witches' covens where they have been known to pray against Christian marriages. Christians who take prayer seriously should always put on the armour of God, ensure there is no sin in their lives and pray for protection. It is also encouraging to remember the verse from Proverbs:

A curse that is causeless does not alight.

(Proverbs 26:2 RSV)

Intercessory prayer

There are different levels of prayer. I spoke about intercession in Chapter 10. This takes prayer to a deeper level, and I believe intercessors are appointed by God. We can think of them acting as shock troops or Special Forces in God's army and as such they may have liberty to take on satanic princes when led to do so by the Holy Spirit.

However, this in no way invalidates the prayers of the saints in general. Such intercessors are simply another part of God's army in the Church. It is also true that all believers can on occasion intercede for a person or situation when called to do so by God, but it is not their normal way of prayer. As mentioned earlier, I have sometimes found myself weeping in prayer over another person or situation but I know that I have never carried the burden in prayer described by God's appointed intercessors. There are good examples of spiritual warfare and intercession in John Dawson's book, *Taking our Cities for God* [5].

There are four other things to mention in relation to prayer: Praying in tongues, fasting, the Blood of Jesus and the prayer walk.

Praying in Tongues

I have already mentioned the baptism in the Holy Spirit. Praying in tongues (*a different language*) is one of the supernatural gifts of the Holy Spirit to believers. This is the gift of an utterance in tongues for the Church which is then interpreted by someone else. This is usually a message of encouragement or warning to the Church and is similar to a prophecy, another of the nine gifts of the Spirit *(1 Corinthians 12 to 14)*. Such a gift is given to certain people to exercise in the Church.

In contrast, I am talking here about the **universal gift of tongues** to believers who have been baptised in the Holy Spirit. It is quite clear that God wants us to use this gift in our daily prayer life. The words spoken are entirely under the control of the Spirit which means we can be certain our prayers are within the will of God. It is a good idea to start our own daily devotions by praying in tongues. It is also appropriate in prayer meetings especially when interceding for people or coming against the enemy. In one prayer group that I lead, someone may say: "Can we all pray in tongues about this person or issue?" We then have a burst of prayer either quietly or out loud until we feel the matter has been dealt with. Praying in tongues like this is an excellent idea in situations where we may not be quite sure how to pray.

Fasting

This is a powerful adjunct to prayer. It can be a simple fast such as missing a meal once a week during a prayer day, to a fast of several days. I do not propose to go into detail here but recommend that people read about fasting before they start to engage in it. People with health issues should certainly do this and may need to take medical advice. God certainly appreciates fasting, and it may be necessary to fast to dislodge demonic forces in certain situations. Jesus himself said as much when the disciples failed to deliver a boy from epilepsy (*Matthew 17:14-20* – see footnote for verse 21).

The Blood of Jesus[6]

It sometimes proves effective and powerful to invoke the blood of Jesus when praying for a person or situation. I sometimes remind the enemy that we have been saved through the shed blood of Jesus and apply this to the person or situation I am praying for. This is another thing that Satan does not like. The book of Hebrews tells us that the risen Christ presented his own blood before the Father in heaven as atonement for the human race (*Hebrews 9:12*). This makes me feel that in some spiritual sense the blood of Jesus is still living and active. However, it is not a weapon that should be used lightly. The shed blood of Jesus is precious to God and to us. Perhaps we should rely on the Holy Spirit to prompt us.

Prayer Walking
This is about claiming territory from the enemy. A church or prayer group may decide to pray for a locality and its residents. It may be that some sin or curse operates in a given locality and that this needs to be broken. Some believers find that praying while they walk around the given area is very effective. Many Christians do not realise that Satan is very territorial. We see this in the gospel story of the Gadarene demoniac. The lead demon (of the legion) begged Jesus not to send them out of the area (*Mark 5:10*). We also learn in the Old Testament that sin and the shedding of blood can defile the land (*Numbers 35:33; Psalm 106:38*). The result is that some areas may be more difficult to evangelise than others. Claiming the territory for God may thus be effective in loosening Satan's grip.

One can see that prayer has many and varied applications. There are several military analogies. Prayer for a neighbourhood or a planned outreach can be considered as **artillery**, softening up the ground. The enemy's hold is weakened before the Word is preached. Fasting before the event can be considered as reinforcement to this artillery.

Intercession can be compared to **close quarter combat**. Paul describes believers as wrestling with the enemy (*Ephesians 6:12*). I think some intercessors would say that such prayer feels very much like wrestling.

Prayer is also defensive as when people pray for other believers who need healing, protection and provision.

8. Binding and Loosing (Binding the strongman)

The practice of binding and loosing divides opinion among believers.

I am firmly of the view that we can and should bind demonic forces, both demons and Satan's angelic forces (strongmen).[7] **However, as I shall explain in Chapter 16, this needs to be done under the Lord's authority and in a disciplined way.** The Hebrew word for bind means to forbid by an indisputable authority, while loose means to permit by an indisputable authority. When one reads the relevant texts in Matthew (*Matthew 12:22-29; 18:18-20*) and then relates them to the texts about binding the strongman, it is quite clear that Jesus is referring to Satan and his kingdom. Furthermore, if we want to plunder the strongman's goods, we must first bind him. Satan's goods are the souls who are held captive by him; so one way to set them free is to bind the satanic forces holding people captive from hearing and understanding the gospel. This calls to mind the scripture from Isaiah spoken to the disciples by Jesus:

> *You will indeed hear but never understand, and you will indeed see but never perceive. For this people's heart has grown dull, and with their ears they can barely hear, and their eyes they have closed, lest they should see with their eyes and hear with their ears and understand with their heart and turn, and I would heal them.*
>
> *(Matthew 13:14-15)*

Given that elsewhere in scripture it is quite clear that God wants all people to be saved (*2 Peter 3:9; 1 Timothy 2:4*), it is not unreasonable to assume that the failure to see, hear and understand the gospel is partly put upon people by Satan. There is indeed wilful human blindness to the things of God (*Romans 2:19-23*), but experience has shown that people can be set free from spiritual blindness by release from Satan's hold. They can then decide whether they want to accept the salvation offered by Jesus.

We can **bind** (forbid) demonic spirits from causing trouble and blinding people to the truth. I believe we can also **loose** God's power through the Holy Spirit into a situation both to disperse the enemy and to bring peace and healing. For example, we can loose the fruit of the Spirit such as faith and hope, where there is unbelief and hopelessness. Where people fall within our remit, such as family and friends, we can bind any spirits attacking or holding them captive. I think this is especially true where we may be the only people praying for or witnessing to such people. I think it is a wise precaution to pray with a prayer partner or for a husband-and-wife team to pray in this way. Should it come to a question of deliverance, then one needs to take the case to the Church elders or experienced prayer team.

When we come to pray for a city area, this needs to be done as a church (See Chapters 15 & 16). We start by asking the Holy Spirit to identify the **strongman** (power) in charge of the stronghold, for example a particular area of a city, an historical event or the shedding of blood. This strongman can be removed by a more powerful strongman in the person of the Holy Spirit. We are simply the agents and must bear in mind the verse from Zechariah:

Not by might, nor by power, but by my Spirit, says the Lord of hosts.

(Zechariah 4:6)

9. Evangelism

Evangelism is the nub of spiritual warfare. It is entirely offensive. We take the battle to the gates of the enemy. This is what all believers are commissioned to do, to extend salvation to as many people as possible and thus to extend the kingdom of God on earth (*Matthew 28:19-20; Mark 16:15-18; Acts 1:8*).

We can liken evangelism to an attack by the **infantry**. However, such an "attack" is not guaranteed to succeed. It may fall on deaf or resistant ears unless the ground has been prepared first. This is where the previous weapons like praise, proclamation and prayer come into play. We are all required to witness to our faith, but some people are called to be evangelists. They cannot fail to speak to people about Christ – the message burns within them.

Powerful and effective evangelism is accompanied by supernatural signs of healing and deliverance from demons. The Holy Spirit is fully at work in such evangelism. The evangelist and his team are fulfilling the commission to spread the word as spoken by Jesus in *Mark 16:15-20*. This was seen in the work of famous twentieth century evangelists such as Smith Wigglesworth and Derek Prince and is also seen today among contemporary evangelists in various parts of the world.

10. Deliverance and healing

When we look at the gospels, we see that Jesus empowered his disciples to bring healing in his name and to set people free from demonic bondage. This still happens in today's Church under the power of the Holy Spirit, but over the centuries the Church at large has lost this capability. Many Christians think that such supernatural signs belonged only to the early Church. However, God kept this activity alive in a remnant of the Church throughout Church history. In the twentieth century the baptism in the Holy Spirit and accompanying gifts burst again upon the Church, first in the Pentecostal Movement and then later in the century in the Charismatic Movement.

Deliverance and healing should accompany evangelistic outreach as it demonstrates God's supernatural power. It is a sign to people that he is real and that the gospel is true. Deliverance is an offensive weapon which rolls back Satan's domain of activity.

However, Christians may find that they need prayer for deliverance and healing after they have been saved. Many Christians find that, despite their conversion and faith in the Lord, they are still bound by things either from their own past or that of their forebears. Freemasonry would be an example of such bondage. Ministries, such as *Ellel* and *Sozo International* in the United Kingdom, have come into being to cater for these needs. These ministries aim to consolidate and protect the lives of believers who have come to faith. In this context such activity could be considered defensive.

In theory the local church should cater for such needs, and indeed some do, but as many churches today do not recognise the supernatural power of God to deliver and heal, para-church ministries have grown up to take care of these needs.

11. Post-conversion care

I have included the follow-up and care of converts as part of God's weaponry. It is purely defensive, but just as an army has to consolidate positions and build defences when it has taken ground, so the Church needs to protect its new converts. It refers to the care of new Christians in a church so that they receive teaching, prayer and fellowship.

It is a great mistake to think that once a person is saved they will automatically bed down and grow into strong Christians. The pull of the world and its attractions can still appeal to our old nature and draw the Christian away from his newfound faith, on top of which Satan is waiting in the wings to do exactly that. Jesus made clear in the parable of the sower (*Matthew 13*) that the seed needs to fall onto good ground if it is to grow up to be productive for the kingdom of God. This good ground is provided by the church environment.

We can liken the new convert to a sprouting seed (such as an acorn) which first grows into a sapling, then into a young tree and finally into a mighty oak. The oak can look after itself, but the seedling and the sapling need protection. Such protection should be provided by the Church. A Church that takes care of its converts will retain them.

12. Covering

I want to close this discussion of the weapons of warfare by looking at the very important subject of covering. Covering is an important concept for the Christian to understand. It is like an overarching defence provided by God. We do not live in neutral spiritual territory. Before we come to salvation in Christ we are in the spiritual territory of our enemy Satan. When we come to faith in Jesus we are transferred to his kingdom (*Colossians 1:13; 1 Peter 2:9*). There is no neutral place between the two spiritual kingdoms.

When we come into God's kingdom we come under his protection or **covering**. *Psalm 91* summarizes this beautifully:

> *He who dwells in the shelter of the Most High will abide in the shadow of the Almighty. I will say to the Lord, "My refuge and my fortress, my God, in whom I trust."*
> *(Psalm 91:1-2)*

We can move to this place of protection, because our sins which separated us from God, are now described as being **covered** by the blood of Jesus. Once in this place of safety we have a responsibility to stay there. If we sin or if we hold on to unforgiveness we open ourselves to attack from the enemy. We are no longer fully covered. One Christian teacher[8] has compared this condition to being covered by an umbrella with holes in it! We can put this right and come back under full covering by confessing sin and ensuring that we have forgiven people who may have harmed us.

Clearly, it is important for all believers who engage in spiritual warfare to examine themselves and make sure their umbrellas no longer have any holes! Satan does not like the Church making war against him and he will seek to exploit any point where God's covering is unable to operate.

The main problem for believers is that they may have been exposed to things in Satan's kingdom before they came to salvation. The Bible is very clear that sins, some more than others, will expose people to the darts of the enemy. One such sin is idolatry. Where their parents or ancestors practised idolatry, such people may have suffered the consequences of this ancestral iniquity. (See: *Exodus 20:4; Deuteronomy 5:8-10*). These sins, along with inadequate parenting, can lead to hurts and wounds in childhood which may get buried and then resurface many years later in adult life. Often this provides an opportunity for the enemy to hold someone in demonic bondage many years after the trauma was experienced. Christian organisations like Ellel Ministries are very experienced in helping believers to deal with these hurts from the past and to set them free to come fully under God's protective covering.

A good idea for believers who want to participate in spiritual warfare teams is to seek help beforehand where they suspect there are unresolved issues. There will be spiritual counsellors in their church and their advice should be sought before going deeper into this. It is important for believers to be as fully under God's protective covering before engaging in spiritual warfare.

Conclusion

We can see from this discussion of offensive and defensive weapons that God has given the Church a considerable armoury. I myself was surprised as I drew up this list to find that it proved so extensive. The challenge now is to get the Church to use this armoury to the full!

NOTES

1. Some believers think that the armour was put in place when we first came to faith. They therefore believe that it is ritualistic to put on the armour each time we engage in warfare. I now disagree: I think the apostle Paul has given us a command each time we wrestle against principalities and powers and other demonic forces. Furthermore, we are reminding God that we take his instructions seriously, and we are reminding Satan that we have done so!

2. The reader who seeks to know more about this baptism should read the scripture passages given in the text. People receive the Holy Spirit at the time of the new birth in Christ (conversion), but they are immersed and empowered by the Spirit when they receive this baptism. It is truly supernatural and the believer usually finds they can pray and give praise to God in a language that has not been learnt. It is a gift from God in which our spirits by-pass our minds.

    For many centuries this experience was suppressed in the Church, a common argument being that it only belonged to the first century AD to get the Church up and running. However, in the twentieth century, it seems that God decided that the Church should embrace it once again and it was revived first in the Pentecostal churches and later in the charismatic movement. Sadly, there are still Christians today who deny the validity of this experience.

    - It is a gift from God, but one that a believer generally has to ask for.
    - It is usually received when other Christians lay hands on a person and pray for him or her to receive the gift.
    - It can be received when praying alone (this happened to the author).
    - It can also happen spontaneously in a church meeting
    - It may sometimes happen simultaneously with salvation, following the prayer of faith.

    The usual sign is that one finds oneself speaking in a new language. It is important to relax and let this happen. Anxiety or attempts to control what is happening may inhibit reception of the gift of the Spirit. The Holy Spirit often does a spiritual work in a believer at the same time which may lead to joyous laughter or tears. It is not to be feared. Any initial excitement settles down within hours or days, but the gift remains.

3. In doing this it should be noted that we are not confessing the sins of other people for salvation, that is something they must do for themselves. What we are doing is to recognise the sins of our forefathers or the nation acting in ignorance, and submit this recognition humbly before God.

4. A very good illustration of the power of repentance is given in the amazing revival in Fiji in the early 2000s. The nation had reached a desperate state of disharmony and poverty where the very land, rivers and sea seemed to be cursed. In July 2001 Christians in Fiji joined together for three weeks of prayer and Bible teaching. At the end of that time, the Prime Minister himself spoke to a crowd of 10,000 and told them of the need to put the nation right in the eyes of God. This led to different churches working together and the creation of Healing the Land teams (HTL) which visited villages one by one to institute fasting, prayer, repentance and spiritual warfare. The teams and the villagers waged spiritual warfare against the enemy, in particular witchcraft and idolatry, in the name of Jesus and through his shed blood. The turnaround has been phenomenal. Land has become fertile, fish have returned to rivers and sea and coral has been renewed, along with major changes in attitude and relationships among the people. To me the most striking aspects of the change were people's repentance for their own sins and confession of those of their forebears, and the unity of the different churches. A full factual account can be read on a website called The Interceders (List of Interceder Encouragers No 14 found at: www.prayforrevival.org. uk)

5. Dawson, John, *Taking our Cities for God* (Florida: Charisma House 2001)

6. Some intercessors (for example Pat Hughes and Gay Hyde in *Helps to Intercession and Warfare*, Chapter 6) disagree with using the blood of Jesus as a weapon. They argue rightly that 'pleading the blood of Jesus' does not feature anywhere in scripture. They argue too, that the function of the blood is to cleanse us from sin and all unrighteousness and not to protect us in spiritual warfare. I disagree somewhat with this view in that I think it is good to remind Satan that Jesus shed his blood for us and for the people we are praying for. I know from experience that Satan's demonic forces do not like mention of the blood of Jesus.

7. I was finally persuaded that 'binding' is meant to be an active command when I read Dean Sherman's account (p195 *Spiritual Warfare for every Christian*) where he describes the horrifying experience of Darlene Cunningham, wife of the founder of YWAM, where she is nearly electrocuted. Her pleas to God are not working and moments before her likely death she cries out to God and receives the words: "Bind the devil, Darlene". The moment she did this she was violently released from the live wire she had accidentally touched.

8. See David Cross' excellent book *God's Covering – A Place of Healing* (UK: Sovereign World 2000)

Chapter 12
Unity: How the Church Becomes a Victorious Army

Introduction

The following four chapters (12 to 15) outline the plans for the Church as an army and the way it should operate. **This is the most novel part of my book and I wish to emphasise that it is not a blueprint for action**. It is a series of ideas and suggestions as to how the churches in a given locality could operate as an army. The essential theme is that the Church should go on the offensive against Satan's kingdom and that it **should do this in a united, organised and disciplined way**. A suggested structure as to how this might operate is the narrative of the next chapter, Chapter 13 **The Churches prepare for battle**. I should feel equally gratified if my ideas provoke Church leaders to consider alternative ways of waging this warfare in their locality.

We saw at the beginning of Chapter 10 the attributes of a victorious military army. In this and the following chapters we are going to see how the Church itself can become a victorious army.

I need to acknowledge that many church leaders do understand about Satan and his kingdom and are waging spiritual warfare. This is particularly true of 'defensive' warfare where they are delivering people from demonic bondage and protecting the flock. Fewer churches will be engaged in 'offensive' warfare where they take the fight to the enemy, so that he is forced to release his captives when they hear the gospel.

We have seen that over the span of history the Church has become fragmented into different denominations and other groups. I believe that God works with the Church as he finds it at any given time in history. It can achieve much, but I believe it does not reach the potential that God plans for a **united Church**. Thus many churches are fulfilling the call to the great commission whether they actively engage with Satan or not. They plant churches, they pray and they hold evangelistic outreaches. Many, many people have come to Christ as a consequence of this over the years. I have been impressed to see that my former church has planted several churches in European towns and elsewhere. My only question would be: do the people called to plant these churches feel they should engage with other churches in the locality, or do they feel this is a mission they can and should do on their own?

Unity among churches

This brings me to the vital question of unity among the churches. Many believers are familiar with *Psalm 133*:

> *Behold, how good and pleasant it is when brothers dwell in unity!*
> *It is like the precious oil on the head, running down on the beard, on the beard of Aaron, running down on the collar of his robes!*
> *It is like the dew of Hermon, which falls on the mountains of Zion! For there the Lord has commanded the blessing, life evermore.*
> *(Psalm 133:1-3)*

The Psalm ends with a blessing, a clear sign that the Lord approves of unity among his people. I would go so far as to say that unity among the churches within a locality is a requirement of the Lord.

Further evidence of the importance of unity is given by Jesus' words in Matthew:

> *If two of you agree on earth about anything they ask, it will be done for them by my Father in heaven.*
> *(Matthew 18:19)*

We tend to think of this verse as referring to two people, but there is no reason why it should not also mean two or more churches. Later, I will address the role of the Church nationally, but for the moment I am addressing the local church. In practice this will mean a collection of churches in a city, town or rural area. In a large city this will mean geographical areas of the city, with manageable numbers of churches. Where a large city is split into such areas it would seem wise to retain a citywide oversight by the denominational leaderships of those churches, which agree to co-operate. I recognise that the situation in Britain is different from that in countries like the United States[1].

Paul and the Corinthians

We need to remember that when Paul went to a city like Corinth, he was addressing all Christians in that city. We get a hint that there were separate groups (forerunners of denominations) in *1 Corinthians* when he says:

> *I appeal to you brothers, by the name of our Lord Jesus Christ, that all of you agree, and that there are no divisions among you, but that you be **united** in the same mind and the same judgment.*
> *(1 Corinthians 1:10)* [emphasis added]

He goes on to criticise those who say: *I follow Apollos; I follow Paul; I follow Cephas (Peter).* He wants none of this division among the believers.

God does not like this fragmentation but, as already mentioned, he accepts its de facto existence as a consequence of history. What we do not know is where the Church would be if this fragmentation had not happened. How much has it impeded the gospel? How much has it prevented effective warfare against the enemy?

We can examine situations where churches in a locality have co-operated well[2] and we can map out the kind of activity a united church could undertake.

Preparing to engage the enemy

What follows applies to churches that have agreed to co-operate in tackling Satan's hold over a city, town or rural area. I realise that not all churches will agree to do this, but it is a good idea to involve as many local churches as possible, especially those which are evangelical and charismatic. In preparing the churches for spiritual warfare, we start with the individual church and finish with their mutual co-operation.

In preparation for the battles ahead I should like to suggest that every church in a locality undertakes to:

1. Understand the Church's principal mission which is to win souls for Christ. Everyone needs to feel they have a part to play in this – it is not restricted to leaders and a few active members. I have always found that older, formerly active members of the church, still love to pray.

2. Subscribe to sound doctrine and faith (see Appendix 1). However, the church does not have to agree on all aspects of doctrine with other churches!

3. Have clear, firm, but humble leadership.

4. Have regular Bible study and prayer meetings. The Pentecostal church I joined as a new Christian nearly fifty years ago, had Tuesday evening prayer and Thursday evening Bible study every week without fail.

5. Also have targeted prayer groups meeting at other times: these might be for their overseas missionaries, particular groups within their community, Israel and so on. Its ability to do this will of course depend on its size. Small churches might cover these particular subjects in their general prayer meetings.

6. Have teaching on Satan's kingdom, purposes and tactics. This might be run as a course in the main Bible study, to be repeated from time to time. For the church setting out on the course of action proposed in this book, it might be a good idea to set up a Bible study specific to this subject, perhaps in co-operation with other churches.

7. Provide good pastoral care and be willing to use specialist Christian organisations where needed. There will be several specific groups such as mums and toddlers, care for the elderly,

students, outreaches to those in need, and these should nest within the church's overall outreach to its community.

Some churches will be doing most of these things already. I am listing them simply to provide a foundation for churches that do wish to engage with other churches with a view to spiritual warfare. I have not specified evangelism separately from mission and I will now explain why.

It is my view that most of a church's evangelism should be done in conjunction with its sister churches in the sort of area we have defined. In my experience a major weakness in Church evangelism is what I call the **centripetal effect**. The Church looks inward to say, "how can we evangelise and win people for Christ?" I think this is the wrong starting point. The Church needs to look outwards.

Working with other churches

I think a church will gain enormously from its willingness to work with other local churches and to step outside denominations for the purpose of evangelism. **I cannot stress how important I think this is**. I am quite sure that when God looks down on his Church in a location, he does not see lots of individual churches, but a body of believers, with different theology and liturgy, yes, but one body. At the moment there is too much of the "lone ranger" mentality!

I live in a conurbation where the Church is fragmented. From time to time the churches get together for an outreach or joint prayer, but it never lasts. I think this pleases Satan no end! I think that churches which work together consistently over a period of time are blessed by God and he uses the outreach and prayer to bring people to salvation.[3]

Planning for outreach

Bearing in mind that Satan seeks to thwart the evangelistic mission of the Church, what should working together look like? I suggest that churches might do the following things:

1. The various church leaders meet and agree to work together over a long period of time – not just for one outreach.

2. They ensure that their theology is on the same wavelength but agree not to let differences in theology and liturgy interfere with their joint activities. Inevitably there will be some self-selection at this early stage. If a minister or existing group of ministers decides to take the initiative in convening a citywide leaders' meeting, some churches with very different emphases may simply decline the invitation. Although churches may not at present work together, the pastors/ministers often know each other and meet informally. They may also meet under the umbrella of a national organisation such as the *Evangelical Alliance* in the United Kingdom[4].

3. They agree to constitute themselves as a leadership team for their city. I think it is wise for the lead pastors to be on this team without exception, however much they choose to delegate thereafter.

4. This team is the **lynchpin of the whole campaign**. It is wise to spend quality time praying, discussing and eventually creating a battle plan for reaching the locality with the gospel message.

5. They need to think about joint prayer teams. I will expand this topic in the next chapter.

6. They need to think about joint evangelistic teams.

The leaders could draw up the plan in the way that an army might draw up a battle plan. They would start by consulting the Holy Spirit in prayer in order to seek the Lord's purpose for the area. They might decide to split into smaller prayer groups and seek the Lord's intent over several weeks or months. **Any warfare must start with the Lord if it is to succeed and be carried out safely.**

> *Many are the plans in the mind of a man, but it is the purpose of the Lord that will stand.*
> *(Proverbs 19:21 See also: Proverbs 16:3 & 9)*

With the help of the Holy Spirit, they would be able to identify enemy strongholds in the city. It would be good to consult believers in the different churches with knowledge of the history of the city (or town/rural area). This would help to identify historical curses in the city, unrighteous covenants and land which may have been defiled through bloodshed. It would be important to identify the powers in control of strongholds in the city, so that when the time is right these can be tackled directly. This would be a simple form of **spiritual mapping.**[5] Depending on what they find, they may decide to divide the city into geographical areas centred on particular churches and then tackle the areas one by one over several years.

Alternatively, they might decide to tackle the city by communities or by strongholds and evangelise this way. There is no one pattern to suit all locations. They could arrange crusades and evangelistic outreaches at appropriate points in their campaigns. If they come fully into tune with the Holy Spirit, he will direct what they need to do step by step as they meet, pray and discuss. He will also indicate the timing of events. I am always struck by the passage in the *Acts of the Apostles* where Paul tried to enter the city of Bithynia in Asia Minor, but the Holy Spirit prevented him from doing so. The reason became apparent during the night, when Paul had a vision calling him to Macedonia (*Acts 16:6-10*). A group of church leaders united in their mission can be led by the Holy Spirit in the same way.

Depending on the size of the location, groups of churches could then be allocated areas for further planning. Whatever the size of the area chosen – the whole city or part of one – the key teams in each area would be the **leadership team** followed by the **prayer** and **evangelistic teams.** My view is that these should always be joint teams.

I do not think we should shy away from such planning because it sounds organised and military – the objective is to become a victorious army, and this is a Christian warfare campaign. I recently heard about an intercessor in the United States. This lady dresses in battle fatigues every time she goes into intercessory prayer. My initial reaction was: this is strange to say the least! However, as I thought more about it, I realised that this was **an expression of intent**. This lady was sending a message to the enemy that she considers her intercession to be warfare; and I concluded that this was an admirable message to send.

I am not recommending this as intercessory dress code or that the rest of us need to do it! What we do need to do, however, is to operate against the enemy with the same intent. That is what is commendable.

NOTES

1. The United States now has many mega-churches comprising thousands of congregants. Many of these people will come from great distances to attend church, not tied to the locality in which the church is situated. Smaller communities in the United States will conform to the traditional pattern in Britain where the churches still tend to serve their local communities. Strategies may be different, but the mega-church can still take on the enemy in appropriate areas. Groups within the mega-church will be able to co-operate with local churches in the areas from which they come.

2. See Chapter 18 for examples

3. My wife and I belonged to a small but committed inter-city prayer group for many years. We prayed for the churches to work together and this occasionally happened. At one meeting, a member of the group was given the following picture which I relate in her own words:

    I had a picture of a football pitch with teams of players all trying to get their own ball into the same goal at the same end of the field. There were many 'goalkeepers/defenders' at this one end of the field, kicking each team's ball back, and not allowing any to get into the goal. Then suddenly there seemed to be a large hand 'herding' all the teams back, so they were all crowded together in the centre of the field.

    I felt the teams represented different churches and the ball was each church's individual programme or agenda. Each church was trying to score its own goal. I felt that it was God's angelic forces stopping each attempt to score and God's hand was pushing them back away from the goalposts and 'herding' them together so they could come together and seek him and discover God's own intentions.

4. Interdenominational national organisations are a good idea. They can bring issues that concern the Church at large to the attention of politicians and other national organisations. They can raise concerns with the relevant people at national level. They are only as effective, though, as the individual churches or denominations choose to make them.

5. **Spiritual Mapping** has had a mixed reception in the Church. Some believers think it has gone overboard in trying to discern the enemy's activity in a town or rural area. This may sometimes be true. However, if one sees it as studying the spiritual history of a locality then it does make eminent sense. Surely it is sensible to discover as much as possible about the historical strongholds of a city. This is a form of military planning: to discover the enemy's strongpoints and why particular sins are prevalent in a locality, before one decides to engage the enemy.

CHAPTER 13
CHURCHES PREPARE FOR BATTLE

In the last chapter we established the principle of operation in the warfare with Satan: co-operation between churches in a locality. I suggested that the three key teams for successful warfare and outreach were:

The leadership team – of lead pastors/ministers

The prayer team

The evangelistic team

and that these teams should all be joint teams.

In this chapter I am going to examine the preparations for battle in more detail. Most churches will have very little experience of the kind of activity I am suggesting. It is therefore necessary to discuss the preparation of individual churches. **As I said at the beginning of Chapter 12, this is not a blueprint for action but rather a suggested framework of ideas to get churches thinking about how they would undertake this activity.**

The joint leadership team is of paramount importance and, once they have agreed to campaign together, they will need to draw up a battle plan, taking into account the factors mentioned in the last chapter. I recognise that pastors are busy people and a new undertaking like this will impose strains. There will be deputising and there will be sub-groups as each church adjusts to the new activity. That is fine; but my point is that the lead pastors must own this activity if it is to succeed[1]. As the US President Harry Truman famously said: *"the buck stops here!"*

I will assume for the sake of argument that the team has decided to wage warfare against Satan by geographical area within the city, town or rural area and to tackle the areas sequentially. This means that the activity at any given time will be centred on the Church in that area[2]. **I stress that this is purely to illustrate how the churches**

need to prepare. The collective leadership may decide early on, under the guidance of the Holy Spirit, that a preferred strategy is to tackle the locality's strongholds rather than work through the locality area by area.

Getting ready

Let us look at what needs to happen in each church before battle commences. We must start by assuming that each church is unprepared for battle. This requires what a military army calls "basic training". Such training is necessary whatever strategy is agreed.

I suggest that the church is told what is going to happen and be enthused with the prospect of bringing people to salvation, including unsaved people among their families and friends.

Furthermore, a number of churches are going to participate and prepare for battle in the same way. When they are ready, some from each church will be working in joint prayer and evangelistic teams; there will also be back-up prayer teams within the church. Since the leadership team has decided to work through the locality by geographical area, the prayer teams will work from each church sequentially to cover this area. The objective of this prayer will be to soften up enemy strongholds, so that prayer can be followed by evangelism, both by individual churches and collectively through a crusade.

It is important to recognise throughout that the 'glue', which underlies the success of this spiritual warfare, **is the co-operation and unity among the churches** (*Psalm 133*).

Opportunity needs to be given to the congregation to discuss and participate in the preparations. Given that the Lord may speak to the church through any individual, the pastors will be advised to lookout for such ideas, but they will of course need to weigh their validity in the usual way (*1 Corinthians 14:29*).

Individual churches

In the last chapter I listed the needs of a local church in preparation for spiritual warfare. One of them was the suggestion of a weekly prayer meeting (open to all the church). This meeting will come to have a pivotal role in the church's warfare. We shall see shortly that the prayer teams will be limited in number, but the church prayer meeting will be an opportunity for the whole church to be briefed on what is happening and to give **overarching prayer protection to all the teams involved**. Such a meeting will have many calls for prayer: for example, existing activities in the church, God's provision for missionaries whom the church supports and so on. However, it should now add **the local joint-church outreach** to these activities. The whole church can now give covering prayer to the teams that are established.

I do not underestimate the upheaval this will cause to a church's routine and activities. This will be an opportunity for each individual church leadership to review its activities and the commitments of its leaders. The church will be entering an agreement with other churches that will take time and resources. Personnel management will be a key part of the principal leader's activity in each church.

Prayer teams

I recommend that each participating church choose two prayer teams. The first is the **offensive prayer team** that will take the warfare to the enemy. This team need not have many prayers or intercessors. A key part of the suggested strategy is that the offensive team **always** acts as a **combined team** from the churches involved. It could be natural for this team to meet at specified intervals (say weekly or fortnightly) in the church whose area is being prayed over and then evangelised.

Suppose four churches are working together in a town or specified locality. If each church contributes five prayer warriors then the offensive team has twenty members, plenty to allow for unavoidable absences.

There is then a second **defensive prayer team** in each church with people who pray for the protection of the main or offensive prayer team. It would be wise to pray at the same time as the main team, but the teams would not necessarily have to meet together. They could all pray in their individual churches. The defensive prayer team could include less experienced people who might later graduate to the offensive team once they are sufficiently experienced.

This idea of back-up teams comes directly from Francis Frangipane's experience of spiritual warfare in the United States[3].

This kind of supporting prayer is akin to "covering fire" in the army when soldiers are ordered to attack an enemy post. While one group of soldiers is attacking, another group is providing covering fire which forces the enemy to keep their heads down.

Serious praying as preparation for evangelism may be new to many church members. However, the thrust of this book is that **prayer and battling against our satanic enemy in a unified way with other churches, is the key to success**.

The praying (which includes praise and many other weapons described in Chapter 11), tackles enemy strongholds and softens up the enemy's defences. If I am right about this, then evangelism should be easier. The church should find that people are more open to the gospel; spiritually hard areas where the church has had little or no impact for many years should begin to soften. Leaflets and public events in the church should yield results.

The offensive team's prayer meeting

According to the scenario just described, the offensive team prayer meeting (be it weekly, fortnightly or monthly) should be the big event for whichever church is under the spotlight. For the churches collectively to own this work, the prayer team must be a joint team. When the work is done and evangelism has taken place, this team, perhaps with a change of personnel, will move onto the next church in the plan[4].

Evangelism

Some believers have a call to evangelism while other just like doing it. Those people should be drawn into the church's evangelistic team. The churches will have to decide collectively how they are going to evangelise. Whereas I think it is essential that churches create a joint offensive prayer team, this may not be so important with evangelism. This will be local evangelism by the church: talking to neighbours, knocking on doors, invitations to gospel services, and then as the work proceeds there will be collective evangelism. There will come a point when the joint leaders may decide it is time for a city to hold a citywide crusade with a well-known evangelist. For such activities the evangelist teams will work together.

Follow-up and after care

Just as some people are called to prayer or called to evangelism, others will be called to pastoral work. **Caring for new converts is of supreme importance**, as they need to be established in the faith and integrated within the church community. Many churches already provide this kind of care, but it will be important to define it and make sure it is providing Bible study, individual prayer, counselling and so on.

Planting new churches

If the process of prayer, evangelism and follow-up is successful then it is quite likely that there will be a need for new churches. It would be an excellent expression of unity if the collective leadership could discuss and agree which church was best suited to plant a new church.

The collective (joint) leadership should never miss an opportunity to display its co-operation and unity. This in itself is a powerful weapon to defeat the enemy.

A note of caution

The enemy will not like all this preparation and activity. The churches need to be warned from the beginning that the enemy will be alerted by this resolve and activity and will soon try to disrupt the preparations. We will examine the enemy's likely response in a Chapter 17, so that the churches can be vigilant. The element of surprise, so characteristic of many human battles, will be missing, but we should not underestimate God's ability to set a few traps for the enemy, as he did in the Old Testament!

Preparatory teaching in the Church

Having outlined the organisational preparation for spiritual warfare, I close this chapter with necessary teaching in each church to prepare it for the coming conflict. This is about making sure that individual believers understand their faith. I would suggest the following teachings:

The **First teaching** will be on holiness and righteousness. In particular, people need to be taught about forgiveness and right relationships. The leaders need to hear from the Holy Spirit if there are things that need putting right in the Church.

The **Second teaching** (which can of course run parallel with the First or other teachings) will be about Satan, his kingdom and his tactics. The members will be taught to watch for his counter attacks and his diversionary tactics. Every person should come out of this teaching understanding the need to put on the armour of God and pray for protection.

The **Third teaching** will be about the kingdom of God and what Christ has done for us on the Cross. The Church may be better prepared on this topic than other subjects. However, everyone needs to have a good understanding about salvation and eternal life. People need to understand the eternal destinies of heaven and hell, depending on whether a person is saved or unsaved. Church members in particular need a sound understanding of the Bible should they become part of the evangelistic teams.

The **Fourth teaching** will be on evangelism, the fundamental activity of the Church as an army. The leaders of the different churches will need to discuss the most appropriate ways of evangelism. These could include: conversations, leaflets, knocking on doors, talking to people in shopping malls, church services, invitations to Alpha or similar courses and periodic crusades. Each campaign (area by area of the locality) could be concluded with a crusade by a well-known evangelist.

The **Fifth teaching** will be on follow-up. People who come to Christ will need to be looked after both socially in the church and in prayer. The church might set up a prayer team solely devoted to praying for new converts and people interested in the faith.

Conclusion

The ideas in this chapter are all **suggestions**, some more important than others. The joint leadership and individual churches will have to decide which ideas they need to implement to create an effective army to wage war against Satan in their city, town or rural area. I have used geographical areas of a city as an illustration of how to wage this warfare, but the collective leadership of churches in many cities may choose an alternative way and seek to evangelise communities within a city. Alternatively, they may seek to concentrate on breaking down strongholds such as witchcraft, paganism, red-light districts or addictions. The collective leadership of the churches are best situated to discuss the alternative for their particular city and then to seek the guidance of the Holy Spirit. In my view, a targeted approach will yield the best results.

NOTES

1. This point of ownership is really important. My experience of inter-church activity is that where a pastor delegates the work to a deputy, rather than attend him/herself, the work often fizzles out.

2. The leadership team may decide that they can select more than one church in a given area at the same time. This will depend on the size of the area undertaken in the campaign.

3. Francis Frangipane *The Three Battlegrounds* chapters 20 & 22. His approach is born out by experience and seems eminently sensible. (Still available from Freedom Publishing)

4. If the strategy is to deal with strongholds one by one, then the team can move on to the next stronghold. I am aware that the situation may not be as straightforward as this: dealing with one stronghold may expose another, linked, stronghold which then has to be dealt with simultaneously.

Chapter 14
Prayer Strategy

Most of this chapter will be devoted to the strategy of the **offensive prayer teams**. Mention of the **defensive prayer team** is made at the end of the chapter. Before we examine how such teams wage war, we need to assess the levels of opposition.

Satan's hierarchy of evil spirits

We have seen in Chapter 5 that Satan directs a kingdom with a hierarchy of angelic ranks. At the lower levels we have the demons who harass humans on earth. The evidence (already referred to) suggests these are not fallen angels. Christians with experience of spiritual warfare report that these demons vary in strength and power, a fact supported by the Bible. Above the demons are the satanic angels who fly in a spiritual realm called the mid-heavens (or heavenly realms) and are grouped according to rank. Paul in *Ephesians 6* gives the principal reference to this hierarchy where he says:

> *For we are not contending against flesh and blood, but against the principalities, against the powers, against the world rulers of this present darkness, against the spiritual hosts of wickedness in the heavenly places.*
> *(Ephesians 6:12 RSV)*
> [The King James version says: *we wrestle not against . . .*]

It is worth dissecting this verse for its meaning. It seems to refer to two categories of fallen angelic spirits: **principalities** and **powers**, the powers being the lesser rank. The remaining two descriptions: *world rulers* and *spiritual hosts of wickedness* would appear to be generic terms covering these principalities and powers. Satan would thus be in control of the principalities who in turn control the powers. These two categories are at the top of the satanic hierarchy. There may be several other categories under these two levels, but this is not clear from the text. What is clear, however, is that the word *hosts* implies there are many of them.

Geographical areas

We can imagine principalities being over empires, nations and perhaps over large cities. Powers would then operate under these principalities. These spirits are thus major spirits over geographical areas of planet earth. This is borne out by the description of the Prince of Persia and the Prince of Greece in *Daniel 10*. The angel Gabriel describes to Daniel how the Prince of Persia withstood him for 21 days until the archangel Michael came to his assistance. It is also borne out by the experience of Christian prayer warriors who have come face to face with such spirits during intercession.

Unrighteous activities

It is also clear that there are major spirit beings in charge of unrighteous activities. Several Christian prayer warriors have identified such spirits, for example Francis Frangipane[1] identifies three major spirits (principalities) as: *Antichrist, Jezebel* and *Babylon*[2]. I would add another, the principality of *Anti-Semitism* whose influence is again on the rise all across the earth.

I am against the practice of some writers naming a whole host of spirits for which there is no clear biblical authority. Some writers think that many characters in the Bible, both human and animal, represent these powers. For example, Goliath and Leviathan represent powerful spirits. John Dawson[3] makes the point that naming spirits out of curiosity can draw unnecessary attention to Satan and his kingdom. He quotes Joshua addressing the Israelites at the end of his life, about the dangers of associating with the surrounding pagan tribes:

You shall not make mention of the names of their gods.
(Joshua 23:7)

My own view is that unless the Holy Spirit reveals the name of a spirit during ministry for deliverance or during prayer warfare, we should not actively seek to name spirits. However, Frangipane does make the point that it is important to know the nature of a spirit during warfare and that in the spirit realm the name of a spirit reveals its nature.

How do principalities and powers operate?

It is important to be clear that the devil and his fallen angels are finite beings. They cannot be everywhere at once in the way that God can be by his Holy Spirit.

In the book of Job God asks Satan what he has been doing (*Job 1:6-8*). Satan replies that he has been going to and fro upon the earth. He has clearly taken note of God's faithful servant, Job. This image of Satan moving about and being limited in his capabilities certainly fits with scenes described in the book *Visions Beyond the Veil*.[4] Here the principalities and powers dwell in the heavenly realm (mid-heavens),[5] but constantly send messengers (lesser angels) to earth with orders to lower beings like demons, who appear to be restricted to the earth. When required, these rulers can themselves come down to earth. It may be then that they reveal themselves to prayer warriors who are battling effectively against Satan's kingdom. The evangelist David Hathaway described how a spirit, describing itself as the spirit (principality) in charge of Russia, revealed itself to David in a statue of Lenin during his first crusade in Siberia. The spirit then spoke to him from the statue[6].

Thus when a pastor comes up against a Jezebel spirit operating in his congregation, he will not be dealing with the Jezebel principality, but one of its lesser spirits – still powerful and to be taken seriously. This spirit in a town or local church might be in command of demons sent to harass people with lust, pride and the undermining of male leadership.

Consequently, it seems reasonably clear from both scripture and experience that there are territorial spirits in charge of geographical areas as well as those in charge of unrighteous activities.

Why is it important to know this?

This knowledge of hierarchy in Satan's kingdom is necessary, because as the reader will see shortly, I believe it is very important that prayer warriors **take on the appropriate opposition**. Just as a platoon of soldiers should not take on a division in a natural army, so a small prayer group should not take on a power or principality over a town or nation. It is what I call the principle of **matching or proportionate force**.

Some prayer warriors will want to challenge this concept, so let me explain why I have come to this conclusion. Such warriors will argue that individuals or small groups of intercessors can take on and displace major principalities. They may quote in evidence the example of Gideon in the Old Testament. The reader will remember that God whittled down Gideon's army to a few hundred men, the angel calling him "a mighty man of valour" (*Judges 6 & 7*). Then there was Jonathan and his armour-bearer who defeated the Philistines (*1 Samuel 14*). In modern times, the intercessor Rees Howells was called with a small band of warriors to intercede for Britain and the allies in the spiritual battles raging over the world during the Second World War.

I recognise that God calls individuals or small groups to do this in intercessory warfare. Such groups can be likened to Special Forces or shock troops in an army. I wrote about intercessory groups in Chapter 10. However, not all battles are like this. There were many full-scale military battles in the Old Testament. Today, in New Testament times, churches working together in an evangelical crusade may fill a whole stadium with praying believers. **Where God has chosen not to use small groups of intercessors, I think it is right to use the principle of matching force.** I think we can find some support for this view from Jesus' own words in Luke, in the parable of the king going to war:

> *Or what king going out to encounter another king in war, will not sit down first and deliberate whether he is able with ten thousand to meet him who comes against him with twenty thousand?*
>
> (Luke 14:31)

I recognise that this parable is about weighing the cost of following Christ, and not about warfare with Satan. Nevertheless, it does reveal that Jesus considered relative strength to be significant.

I believe that the Lord wants the Church to behave as a united and disciplined army, particularly in the last days before Christ's return.

Potential dangers

When an individual or a small group starts to wage war without the green light from the Lord they are in real danger. They are stepping out from under God's protective cover. Satan knows his legal rights and will take full advantage to strike back with illness, accidents and even death. Experienced prayer warriors know this and warn of the dangers of taking on principalities and powers without God's approval. Francis Frangipane, Jennifer LeClaire and others warn that these principalities and powers are not to be trifled with; they have real power to harm us.[7]

Levels of operation

What might matching forces mean in practice? I believe our authority to war against the enemy corresponds to the boundaries of our geographical domain and **the unity practised within that domain**. Modern-day armies have a hierarchical structure ranging from the section of a few men, through the platoon, company, battalion, brigade, division, corps and finally the army. By this time, it has grown to many thousands of troops.

It is customary for battles to be waged with forces of matching sizes. Thus a platoon might take on a section. A whole brigade does not waste its time or resources taking on a platoon, but more importantly a platoon does not try to take on a significantly larger unit. There are exceptions: there are battles where small units have successfully routed much larger units. This was true in the Old Testament and is also true of modern warfare, but it is not the norm.

The Church does not have anything like such a hierarchical structure as an army, though some of the state churches, such as Catholic and Anglican appear to emulate such a hierarchy! The fundamental unit in the worldwide Church is the **local church** and above that is the **national Church**. By local church I mean the whole body of Christ in a city, town or defined rural area. As mentioned earlier, when the apostle Paul wrote to the church at Corinth he wrote to it as a single unity. In reality there may have been several local church groups. This is why I emphasise that the individual local churches in an area (keen to engage in spiritual warfare) **need to work together as though they are one church.**

This is doubly important because Satan by contrast, is both territorial and hierarchical. He is also highly legalistic which means he knows his rights and what, through human sin and iniquity, belongs to him.

The limits of a church's operation

My thesis is that the Church needs to learn what it can legitimately take on and conquer in terms of Satan's realm.

Territorially, each individual church is an outpost with potential authority to rescue Satan's captives within its geographical domain. We can expect to rescue the captives, but not to wrest control of the territory from Satan; that will only happen when Christ returns to overthrow Satan himself [8].

However, the churches in a locality, united in their determination to wage war against Satan, are in a legitimate position to wage war against the principality and powers over their city. In my view they are not in a position to take on the principality over the nation. They are, however, an **appropriate** force to deal with citywide satanic activity.

A cautionary tale

I remember hearing about a man who came into knowledge of spiritual warfare combined with knowledge of Christ's victory over Satan on the Cross. He then decided to climb a hill above where he lived and to bind the powers operating in the heavenly realms above his town. He later described how he felt a dark presence come down around him and how his life then began to fall apart. He lost his job, became severely ill and his marriage may also have broken up. Satan does not like the presumption of such an attack and hit back hard. I think we can also surmise that God did not like this presumption either, which is why he allowed him to suffer the consequences. Eventually, however, God used this experience to bring the man to a place where he did understand his authority and could use it effectively for the kingdom.[9]

Our authority for prayer

At the time of the incident this man did not understand about a proportionate response and the limits of individual authority. As an individual, his authority extended to his family. I believe, provided he had dealt with unrighteousness and unforgiveness in his own life, that he had the authority to bind any spirits attacking his wife, children and other close members of his family as well as people the Lord had called him to witness to or pray for.

Were he the designated or recognised leader of a prayer group within a church, then he and the group would have had the authority to bind spirits relating to the group's realm of prayer. For example, in a missionary prayer group, they could disarm and bind spirits harassing the missionary families they supported. They could not however disarm and bind the principalities and powers operating over the countries where the missionaries worked. Had this man been the pastor of a church then he and the other leaders within the church could have bound the spirits and associated powers operating in the immediate vicinity of his church.

We can thus see the beginnings of a spiritual hierarchy as to how the church might operate against Satan's kingdom.

Summing up

I should like to close this section with two further points. The first is that operating within a correct (and not presumptuous) authority does not mean that Satan will not hit back. This is a war and God lets us experience it, but if we are operating correctly we will have the weapons to protect ourselves and to counter such attacks successfully. The second point (to which I have already referred) is that there is one situation where an intercessor or small group can take on principalities and powers and that is where they are directed to do so by Christ himself through his Holy Spirit.

Warfare at the city level

We can now see why it is so important that churches act together in unity in cities, towns and rural areas. When the churches in a locality are fully prepared (as per the last chapter) and decide to work together, they can then take on and disarm the satanic powers in charge of their town or city. Furthermore, they can also operate against other evil powers operating within the area. For example, although freemasonry is a national movement, they can pray for the local lodge: that masons will be set free to accept Christ and come out from freemasonry. They can war against red-light districts, witchcraft and any other spirit trying to control people's lives within the churches' working domain. They can war against historical curses on the city or things that have defiled the land.

This kind of warfare is rarely seen, but if it was then I believe that thousands of people could be set free to receive the gospel. Not everyone would turn to Christ – we all have free will to accept salvation or refuse it. This means that Satan's activities would continue, but at a much-diminished level. Whole communities can change as witnessed by the Welsh Revival in 1904.

Warfare at the national level

Much prayer goes up for a nation like Britain and the United States, but not much warfare. There are pockets of believers who are called to intercede for the nation on specific issues. Until quite recently, there was a spiritual battle going on in Britain to achieve Brexit (Britain leaving the European Union – see Appendix 5). This was an enormous spiritual battle because Satan was challenging the British people's decision to leave the E.U.

Many believers understand the spiritual nature of the conflict and believe that God has ordained Britain's leaving, but not without a spiritual fight. They believe that Britain needs to come out from under the yoke of the principality over a united Europe. Only then can Britain fulfil God's destiny for this nation. This principality is a major one, because we can trace the origins of the European Union back to the Roman Empire, the fourth great empire described in the book of Daniel[10]. We have reason to believe from the Bible that this empire will be significant in the time before Christ's return to earth.

National days of prayer

Most of the Church is unaware of the spiritual significance of leaving Europe. However, some evangelical leaders have come together to call National Days of Prayer. In the absence of most of the traditional Church, I think these leaders legitimately constitute a national leadership. As such I think it is quite in order for them to take on the principalities and powers that sought to prevent us leaving the European Union. They have done this by asking the assembled company[11] to sing, praise, proclaim the scriptures, and pull down strongholds with prayer and fasting.

I lead a local, very dedicated prayer group of 10-15 people which meets monthly and prays to consolidate *Brexit* as well as praying for the nation in other directions. We do not take on principalities and powers as such but ask God to send his angels to deal with them and all other opposition to leaving Europe. In my view that's as far as a local group should go, unless specifically directed otherwise by the Holy Spirit. I believe our prayer answers God's call and forms part of the mosaic of prayer that ascends to heaven over this issue. The book of Revelation tells us that these prayers are gathered into bowls before God's throne (*Revelation 5:8*).

Back-up or defensive prayer teams

The work of these teams is to provide protection (covering fire in military terms) while the offensive team is at work. Their principal role will be to pray for individuals and their families in the frontline prayer group. There needs to be regular communication between the two groups so that the back-up group is aware of any additional needs for which they should pray. The various church back-up groups can meet in their own churches unless it is deemed a good idea to meet collectively.

We have already seen that the offensive prayer team needs to consist of experienced prayer warriors who have undergone further training for the warfare they are about to undertake. The back-up team is a wonderful opportunity for new people to learn about spiritual warfare without engaging in it directly. At suitable times they can graduate to the frontline team. This group is also an opportunity to prepare for joining other prayer groups that may already exist within the church.

NOTES

1. Francis Frangipane has experienced real battles with the satanic kingdom. He describes some of this in his excellent book *"The Three Battlegrounds"*. He describes his encounter with the Jezebel spirit in Chapter 19.

2. For these particular spirits there is enough biblical evidence to identify them as three major principalities. In fact, antichrist is described as a spirit in the Bible (*1 John 4:3*).

3. Dawson, John, *Taking our Cities for God*, p119

4. This book was mentioned earlier in Chapter 5. *The Kingdom of the Devil*, Chapter 7 in H.A. Baker's book is very interesting in this respect.

5. The passage from *Ephesians 2:1-10* makes interesting reading. It explains how believers in a **spiritual sense** are now situated with Christ Jesus in the heavenly realm, from where they can exercise their God given authority.

6. *Why Siberia? P.115*: someone reading David Hathaway's account of this encounter with the alleged spirit over Russia, may be surprised by the fact that David alone took authority over the spirit in the name of Jesus, breaking its power. I think we must see this occasion as one led by the Holy Spirit in which David, as leader of the Crusade, was given this authority. Before this incident, he and his co-workers had been in intercessory warfare for an hour and David felt prompted to stay behind when the others left.

7. Francis Frangipane reveals his frightening encounter with the spirit of Jezebel in *The Three Battlegrounds* Chapter 19, pp. 136-139.

8. Dominionists would dispute this statement. They argue that if the majority of the people in a community become Christians, then the territory is now under Christ's rule. One would certainly expect a change in the spiritual atmosphere, but the Bible makes clear that Satan is not going to lose control of the earth until Jesus returns at the end of the Tribulation, by which time the world will be in a terrible state.

9. A friend heard this story from the man himself when he was teaching at a well-known ministry for healing and deliverance. He was illustrating from his own life the importance of waging spiritual warfare under God's authority.

10. *Daniel 2* describes Nebuchadnezzar's vision of an enormous statue made of gold, silver, bronze and iron. The different parts and metals describe four great empires, the last being the Roman Empire. *Chapter 7* describes Daniel's own dream in which he sees four great beasts. The last beast represents the Roman Empire, which later transforms into the terrifying future kingdom of the Antichrist.

11. Several thousand believers attended a National Day of Prayer at the SSE Arena, Wembley in West London on 26 January 2019 and at another meeting held on 31 August 2019.

CHAPTER 15

WARFARE IN PRACTICE

I emphasise that this chapter is not meant to be prescriptive. Nevertheless, having written so much about preparing for this warfare, it would be unreasonable of me not to give the reader some idea of what it might look like in practice.

Preparation

The joint leadership team will have chosen an experienced offensive prayer team leader and the men and women who will join this leader. Given most churches' lack of experience in spiritual warfare it is unrealistic to expect to find many prayer warriors with such experience. However, they should be mature people, used to praying in groups.

The leader will have needed to meet with the members beforehand to ensure that they have resolved any issues around unforgiveness or even unconfessed sin. These are the frontline troops and Satan will be on the lookout for any weakness in their armour. The defensive prayer team(s) can be less experienced and the prayer they offer can be looked upon as training. However, they too should have dealt with any potential blockages, such as unconfessed sin and the need to forgive.

1. SPIRITUAL WARFARE – THE PRAYER MEETING

Members of the team may have prepared for the meeting by fasting beforehand or on the day itself.

Praise and worship
The meeting should always start with praise and worship, declaring the greatness of God and what he has done. I sometimes provide song sheets but also allow the members of the prayer group to

choose songs spontaneously. A single instrument like a guitar (but not a group) might also be helpful.

The worship should continue for a while to allow the Holy Spirit to come among the group. The leader will sense this and know when to move on. The Bible tells us that Satan does not like the spiritual light of God, so worship and adoration both honours the Lord and puts Satan on the back foot.

Put on the armour of God
It is noteworthy that immediately after *Ephesians 6:12* where Paul tells us whom we are contending with, that he also tells us to put on the whole armour of God. My wife and I now declare out loud each day that we are putting on the whole armour of God and work through the six items. I certainly think the prayer team should do this immediately after the time of praise.[1]

Asking the Holy Spirit to take charge
There needs to be a time of sharing over what they are likely to be praying about and this is probably best after the time of worship. The group leader then needs to ask the Holy Spirit to take charge, and to recognise that the Spirit may give words of prophecy, knowledge and guidance to anyone within the group. These need to be weighed before returning to prayer. The leader could ask the Holy Spirit to confirm the guidance to other members of the group. However, it is worth pointing out that, as the team become united over time, they will also come to trust each other's spiritual judgement.

Waiting on the Lord
As mentioned in Chapter 11, this is perhaps the most important part of the meeting. We have all the weapons to hand that the Lord might want us to use, but we may be surprised at this stage to find exactly what he wants us to do. If we have not done it already, he may want us to repent and forgive, before he takes us any further into the battle. He will want us to be fully prepared and fully protected. He may well bring us to a state of quiet and peace before he starts to reveal any information.

It is quite in order to ask the Lord to indicate against whom we are waging war, but he may not want us to rush in and bind strongmen and other spirits. Instead he may bring scriptures to mind that he wants us to proclaim out loud. He may burden us to pray in the Spirit for someone or some situation relevant to the subject of our prayers. Do not be surprised if an individual starts to weep or perhaps gets angry in prayer. However, it is very important for the team leader to discern what is going on at every stage of waiting on the Lord and in other parts of the meeting. Prayers can unwittingly lead the meeting off track and the leader must be ready to draw them back in the direction of the Holy Spirit's leading.

As the team prays together, they will find that they become sensitive to the leading of the Holy Spirit and become knitted together. It is in the early days of the team's meetings that the leader will need to be especially vigilant.

Proclamation of scripture

At this point it may be appropriate to declare or proclaim scriptures relevant to the topic of prayer. These may have been revealed while waiting on the Holy Spirit or people may have come with scriptures the Lord has given them beforehand. I usually ask prayer groups to stand while we do this. One person reads the scripture in manageable portions and the rest of us then repeat it. By doing this we are declaring the scriptures into the heavenly places. We can be sure that Satan's angels and demons will be listening in! Team members may also want to read verses or short scripture passages as the meeting proceeds.

Disarming the enemy

At an appropriate time, the leader can proclaim that the inter-church prayer team has authority to **disarm** Satan's powers over the city and that they are now **binding** them over the local area, the red-light district or whatever stronghold they are taking on.

I believe it is very important to be specific at this stage and to deal with one thing at a time. One may have liberty to roam in prayer, but it is quite likely that the Holy Spirit will throw light on particular issues in the area or stronghold in question. The leader should discourage any tendency to jump from one subject to another. The leader can ask the team whether they feel the prayer is complete before moving on. Sometimes just one person may feel that more prayer is needed.

Once people are into Spirit-led prayer they should not feel anxious if they start to weep or to get angry. This is a good sign, as it indicates that the Spirit is at work – it may be particularly evident when a person is praying in tongues. When the emotion lifts, it will also indicate the prayer is complete.

The name and blood of Jesus

Every instruction to the enemy should be made **in the name of Jesus**, as should any request to God. It is also good to invoke **the blood of Jesus**. For example, we may tell the enemy that we are praying for people whose salvation has been purchased by the precious, shed blood of Jesus Christ. One might quote a passage of scripture such as *Hebrews 9:12-14; 10:19-20*.

Some Christians "plead" the blood of Jesus over a person or situation; while not exactly scriptural it is in fact much the same as I am suggesting. Occasional and **respectful** use of the blood of Jesus is an effective weapon because Satan does not like the subject. The shed blood of Christ is what defeated Satan at the Cross (*Colossians 2:15*).

Binding and loosing

I dealt with binding and loosing at some length in Chapter 11 as one of the weapons available to us as warriors. I recognise that believers have different views on this subject. However, I firmly believe that this is an **active** command from the Lord and that it is right to bind the strongman and other demonic forces as part of our spiritual warfare. However, we should first seek the Holy Spirit's guidance and we should not attempt to bind principalities and powers beyond our remit. In other words, a team praying for its local area or particular stronghold should not take on the principality over the nation.

Once the Holy Spirit has revealed the strongman (power) over the area or stronghold for which they are praying, then I believe it is in order for the team leader to remind the enemy that what is bound on earth is also bound in heaven. The prayer partners can then proceed to bind the demonic forces and release the captives, as they feel led.

As well as binding I think we can also loose the qualities of God and the fruit of the Spirit into a place or situation. For example, one might loose God's conviction of sin, repentance and righteousness into a red-light district. Alternatively, one might loose God's comfort, peace and love into situations/places where people have been harmed or abused. (Relevant verses: *Matthew 12:28-29; 16:19; 18:18-20; Mark 3:27* and *Galatians 5:22-23*).

Matching or proportionate force

A major theme of this book has been the use of proportionate force in spiritual warfare just as one would do in a natural war. I believe that the offensive prayer team (if it has been set up correctly) can bind the principality and powers over a town. The churches have agreed a strategy and disarming or binding the ruling spirits over the town is a legitimate act of spiritual warfare.

However, there will be situations where one asks God to do something. For example, the Bible does not say that we can summon or call down angels, but we can actually ask God to send angelic reinforcements. One of my Israel group's frequent prayers is to ask God to send angels to protect Israel's borders.

Let us take an example at the local level: the team might feel led to pray about something nationally, perhaps an undesirable new law being presented to Parliament. Here I think we should ask God to prevent the bill being passed into law. I do not think a local group should try to bind the principality or power behind this law. (At a national level, however, I believe that it would be appropriate to bind such a satanic power).

Praying in harmony

Thus as the meeting progresses, hopefully under the guidance of the Holy Spirit, prayer will entail proclamation, binding and loosing, addressing the enemy directly and asking God to do things. There should be a flow of prayer, back and forth, people sensing when to come in and when to hold back. **Prayers should normally be short and to the point**. The only exception to this that I can envisage is when the Holy Spirit has put a particular burden on one of the team and the rest of the team feel constrained to hold back. Be prepared for God to bring the meeting to a holy silence.

Naming spirits

As the enemy resists, the Holy Spirit may name the resisting spirit[2] and this spirit should then be addressed by name, bound and told to go. The person praying may feel a holy anger. However, we should never demean or insult the enemy. There is a very clear reference to this in Jude (*Jude 9*) where the archangel Michael rebukes Satan but does not rail against him[3].

Collective prayer in tongues

I find in meetings that someone will suggest a time of collective prayer in tongues. If this seems right then we will stand and do this, varying the volume depending on how the Spirit leads us. This is very effective because the Holy Spirit then has free reign to orchestrate the prayer. Once again members may experience righteous anger or weeping as the Spirit leads them into warfare.

An individual should only pray out in tongues if they feel they may have a message (requiring interpretation) from the Holy Spirit. Loud use of tongues when other people are praying quietly can be disruptive.

Repentance and confession of sin

The application of this will depend on the circumstances but bear in mind that one cannot do this individually for people who are actually capable of repenting for their own sin.

During national days of prayer, participants may feel it is right to confess the sins of the nation. In this respect they are representing and confessing on behalf of people now dead or living people who as yet are unaware that they need to confess their own sin. This practice is quite biblical as I demonstrated in Chapter 11. A further well-known verse authorises believers to pray for a nation. This is a good verse with which to start collective repentance:

> *If my people who are called by my name humble themselves, and pray and seek my face and turn from their wicked ways, then I will hear from heaven and will forgive their sin and heal their land.*
>
> *(2 Chronicles 7:14)*

Believers can confess the sins of the nation and ask God to turn from judgement to mercy. This is addressing God in his relationship to the nation and it can be very powerful. A nation that is heading the wrong way can be turned around by the heartfelt repentance of God's people. This in turn can favour the spread of the gospel, so that individuals make their own repentance as they accept Christ as Saviour.

The local situation
Turning now from the national to the local situation, I think we can apply these verses concerning repentance to the areas where we live and the strongholds existing in the city. There may for example, be representatives on the team of families who have lived in the city, town or countryside for generations. I believe it would be very appropriate for them to lead these prayers of repentance for their locality. The team might have former drug or alcohol addicts: again it would be appropriate for them to lead such prayers of repentance.

Prayer walking
So far I have treated the prayer team as meeting in a church. However, it may decide to combine this with prayer walks around the area they are praying for. This should of course be done discreetly in areas of potential danger, such as red-light districts, unless the Holy Spirit indicates that he wants a very public witness.

2. AFTER SPIRITUAL WARFARE

The consequences of spiritual warfare
The objective of this spiritual warfare is the diminishing of sin and a harvest of souls for the kingdom. At some point the churches and the public are going to become aware of positive changes in their communities. The leaders will have to decide when and how to handle the publicity surrounding this.

Other teams in the churches such as evangelism and after care should be making preparations for handling the changes that occur. There will be a new interest in spiritual matters. People will start to ask questions and the teams need to be ready. Satan will also be active, raising voices against what is happening, but we will deal with that in Chapter 17.

On-going prayer meetings
I personally favour a time limit on prayer meetings, so members know what to expect and can plan accordingly, but I do recognise that if the Holy Spirit is flowing, a time limit is not always appropriate.

Opportunity should always be there for people to leave at the expected time when a leader decides to let the meeting continue. Usually the leader will sense a "drawing to a close" and members may well feel that something has shifted in the heavenly places.

However, the team has been set up to achieve an objective and this objective of bringing people in a community to Christ, will not be achieved in one meeting. The offensive prayer team will continue to meet until there is a real sense of breakthrough and the leadership team feels it is time to move elsewhere.

After each meeting they will need to debrief and reflect on what happened. The team leader should report to the leadership team and compare notes with the leader(s) of the defensive prayer teams. They too may have had rewarding time as they prayed for the protection of the offensive team and their families.

When the offensive team meets again, they may find that the enemy has battened down the hatches and built some defences. For example, there may be voices raised against the local church or opposition from within the church to the proposed campaign. This should not dishearten them. Natural warfare involves gains and losses and in spiritual warfare the enemy seeks to undermine the prayer warriors' faith. The defensive team(s) can make a point of asking the Holy Spirit to reveal anything that needs dealing with. If an offensive warrior becomes ill or family issues prevent him/her attending, then the defensive team can zero in on this. As in military warfare, there need to be good channels of communication between different parts of the army. The attitude among all warriors, defensive as well as offensive should be: "we will not let the enemy get away with anything!"

Progress in warfare

The teams should not be disheartened if nothing seems to be moving after some weeks of this warfare. It is a good idea to ask the Holy Spirit to give them some little signs of encouragement, pending the expected breakthrough. Perhaps family members who have fallen away from the faith start coming to church. Perhaps the local pornography shop or abortion clinic closes through lack of business. I believe that God understands the need for encouragement during a warfare campaign. If we ask him, he will provide it (*Luke 11:9-10*). Finally, prayer warriors should remember that theirs is a noble task: they are battling to save souls from hell!

NOTES

1. I mentioned in Chapter 11 when discussing the weapons of our warfare that believers have different views on the 'putting on' of the armour of God and also on the application of the blood of Jesus. In this book I express my conclusions on both these subjects, but readers must come to their own views.

2. It is generally believed by Christians who have engaged in deliverance or in spiritual warfare that demons have names and that the names reflect their nature. Thus the demons plaguing the Gadarene demoniac were known as "Legion" because there were so many of them. Jesus himself asked the demon its name and the head demon answered him. Addressing the demon by its name does seem to add power to the process of expelling it from an individual or binding its activity in a place or situation. It is therefore legitimate to seek the demon's name either from the Holy Spirit or by asking it directly. I have indicated elsewhere that I am not in favour of naming and classifying demons. In my view names should be known on a 'need to know' basis.

3. When we think of the evil Satan has perpetuated among the human race, this limitation may seem strange. However, God's universe is very ordered and legal in the way it works. His angels, and the human race in turn, have been given authority in their domains of activity. For example, Adam was given dominion over the earth and told to rule over all the other creatures (*Genesis 1:28*).

   Likewise Satan was given immense authority as I explained in Chapter 5. We know that he sinned and fell from this exalted position, but in some way that I do not yet understand, he still has some authority. This will presumably cease when he is finally thrown into the Lake of Fire.

   Some teachers believe that Satan was an archangel on a par with Michael and perhaps Gabriel. The passage from Jude shows that Michael could rebuke Satan in the name of the Lord, but do no more. Satan was clearly claiming the body of Moses on the grounds that the human race was now captive to him. However, God was not permitting his favoured servant to be taken this way and sent Michael to deal with the matter.

CHAPTER 16
AN UNDERGROUND CHURCH

This chapter is written for the Western Church which is still free to worship and preach the gospel. It would be presumptuous of me to write as though I have anything to offer that part of the Body of Christ which experiences persecution, and even martyrdom, in many countries in the world and which may have operated underground for many years.

However, this chapter is a necessary addition to my original manuscript. The coronavirus pandemic has brought home to Bible believing Christians first, that we are likely to be heading into the last days before the return of Jesus Christ[1] and secondly, that it is easy for governments, even democratic ones, to close down churches when there is a national crisis. This means that the Church, even in western countries, may have to operate underground in the coming years.

Going underground is not a new idea. Parts of the Church have been underground since the first century after its formation. In much of the twentieth century the Church had to operate underground in different countries at different times – for example, the evangelical church in Nazi Germany and then in Russia and the communist countries.

The Persecuted Church

Today Christians in many countries are suffering persecution. A number of Christian organisations both monitor and organise support (prayer and practical) for persecuted Christians across the world. These organisations include, among others: *Open Doors, World Wide Monitor* and the *Barnabas Fund*. The extent of persecution is truly horrific and increasing year by year. Most of us in the western churches (and I include myself) have little idea as to the extent and degree of persecution. Open Doors produces an annual list of countries which ranks the severity of persecution that Christians face for actively pursuing their faith. This covers 50 countries and ranges from extreme persecution (circa 10), to very high persecution (circa 25) and high persecution (circa 15)[2].

North Korea has topped the list for 20 years. It is difficult to assess the numbers of Christians in North Korea. The penalty for discovery is to be executed or sent to a labour camp where conditions are so severe that few believers make it out alive. It is estimated that up to 70,000 Christians are currently imprisoned in North Korea. Christians have to keep their faith entirely hidden. According to Open Doors there are stories of husbands and wives not knowing for many years that their spouse was also a Christian. Children are encouraged to report to teachers any sign of faith in their parents.

Satan seeks to persecute the Church and to stop the spread of the gospel. He has done this in different ways throughout history, but in the twentieth century his principal way has been to shift governments from democratic norms to anti-Christian dictatorships. He then operates through the state's repressive structures. The Church either has to conform, which means diluting its Christian message, or go underground.

The twenty-first century is no different. There is marked persecution of the Church in non-Islamic countries like North Korea, China and India. What is new however, is the rise of extreme Islam which denies the practice of other faiths and in particular Christianity. The persecution is aimed particularly at converts from Islam to Christianity. Thus Iran is really harsh towards converts from a Muslim background, but protects Christians from the Armenian or Assyrian communities, although treating them as second-class citizens. More Christians are murdered for their faith in Nigeria by independent groups such as Boko Haram, than in any other country. Other Muslim countries which treat Christians harshly include Pakistan, Afghanistan and Somalia.

Persecution of the Church is a huge and distressing subject and further discussion belongs to a different book. The point of this brief description is that the western Church can no longer assume that it is safe from persecution.

What has been happening to the Western Church?

In the western democracies in the twentieth century the evangelical Church has been free to operate even where the official Catholic Church has played a dominant part in the state – such as Italy, Spain and France. This continues into the twenty-first century, but things may be about to change.

Since World War II public respect for and acceptance of the Church with its Christian message has fallen away. Both European countries and the United States have become more secular. Much of the Church has responded to this falling away by diluting the gospel and preaching a social gospel. This emphasises God's love as all embracing, but plays down his holiness and need for repentance and forgiveness of sin through the shed blood of Jesus.

Furthermore, Satan has been singularly successful at infiltrating the Church's hierarchy with non-biblical ideas, and with people who hold these ideas. This is particularly true of the Anglican and other mainline denominations in the United Kingdom and the United States but is also beginning to occur in the Roman Catholic Church[3]. Many ministers are now homosexual or lesbian and the gay cohort of clergy and laity is now pushing the gay and transgender agendas contrary to God's Word on these matters. Where is God's view of marriage being preached in many churches these days? Where is the Church's voice today on the sin of abortion?

Society turns away from Christian belief

As society turns away from Christian belief and values and the Church tries to counteract this by compromising its beliefs and standards, the evangelical Church faces a real danger. Society can reach a tipping point where the authorities can restrict the Church's activities because such activities and beliefs no longer have public support. This tipping point is where the recognised Church has to conform and become the docile servant of the state (as has happened in China) or it has to go underground. Such a time may not be far off, even for countries such as Britain with its fine history of freedom to believe and of taking the gospel across the world.

What is an underground church?

The term *underground* probably emanates from the resistance movements that grew up in many countries in the Second World War. Essentially it means the Church operates in secret, hidden from public view and in particular from government surveillance. For most of communist China's existence the true evangelical Church has had to operate underground. This is increasingly so as the authorities (Communist Party) use the coronavirus pandemic to establish more and more surveillance (street cameras) and to use health ID to turn China into the sort of state described by George Orwell in his iconic book *Nineteen Eighty-four*.

To oppose the unbiblical ideas of much of the Church is to put oneself or one's local church outside the mainstream view. This isolation of the faithful Church has been preceded by a careful satanic strategy to bring the non-religious public onside for the acceptance of alternative lifestyles. This further softens up the Church to accept alternative ways to God and thus embrace other religions. In doing so they forget Christ's words:

> *I am the way, the truth and the life. No one comes to the Father except through me.*
>
> *(John 14:6)*

This puts the faithful Church in real danger and while the Tribulation[4] may still be some time away, we can see the scene being set for Christians to be marginalised in Western society and the true evangelical Church (in many denominations) to be closed down in its public manifestation.

Of course, the true Church will not close – God will keep it going – but it may have to go underground and operate very differently.

How does the underground Church compare with a conventional resistance movement?

There are many similarities between a military resistance movement and an underground church, but also one big difference. The Church has to operate in secret, **but it retains its power with God.** A military underground movement on the other hand is relatively weak. It does not have the wherewithal to challenge the forces of the state or an occupying power either in terms of personnel or weaponry. What it does have is secrecy and surprise in its operations. In World War II many resistance movements paved the way for conventional forces.

For example, the French resistance movement was very effective in damaging the resources available to the Germans: they blew up bridges, derailed trains, destroyed weapons and above all supplied intelligence to the allies as the regular armies came ashore on D-day in 1944. Nevertheless, the battle had to be won by the allies' formal armies. Only in Yugoslavia did the resistance movement grow into a force strong enough to expel the German army by itself.

When the Church goes underground, God operates differently from the way he does through an open and established Church. God remains just as powerful, but he has allowed Satan to be more in control of the state and even to suppress or severely restrict the activities of the Church. A classic case is China (referred to above) where the Three Self Patriotic Movement (Church) is in effect an arm of the Chinese Communist Party which decides what the Church can do and say[5]. This contrasts with the underground Church which today is increasingly persecuted, but which has seen enormous growth of believers in China over the last few decades.

Satan motivates the state to suppress true Christian activity, but counter-intuitively this can release God's power in a way not seen in the Church which operates openly with the state's blessing. In the twenty-first century we have already seen the Church mercilessly persecuted in the countries mentioned above, but we have also seen amazing growth in numbers of believers.

Loss of God's power in the established churches

As people move away from belief in God and in the Christian message in particular, the established churches seek acceptance by watering down the gospel of salvation. They seek ways to become and remain socially acceptable to a less and less interested society. This is exactly what we have witnessed in western nations such as Britain. To remain what they think is relevant, the churches increasingly preach a social gospel rather than a gospel of repentance from sin. This departure from God's Word means that the Church loses its power as the Holy Spirit draws back.

When state repression and public indifference reach a certain level, the underground Church has to become underground for the very reason that it continues to preach a gospel of repentance from sin through Jesus Christ. Unlike the formal Church, it retains God's power and the weapons we have described earlier in this book. It has to operate in secret, but it retains all the power to achieve God's purposes here on earth. God responds to prayer, praise and fasting just as effectively as when the church operates openly.

How can the underground church fulfil its mission?

As I see it, there is no reason why the underground church cannot wage war against Satan's kingdom in the same way that the open church can do as described in the earlier chapters of this book. The big difference is that it has to operate in secret and thus protect itself from betrayal.

Here we find a convergence with the military underground movements in wartime. One of the prime concerns is to protect the movement from external penetration and betrayal from within. Satan cannot simply disclose the location of a secret church or its members. He has to plant human spies or work on grievances among existing members who then betray the group to the authorities.

This means the underground churches would be wise to set up the kind of cellular structures whereby each cell only knows the members of their own cell. The leader does not have contact with members of any other cell. The cells should be limited in size so that if a leader or a member is caught only a few people are at risk.

The leaders will have to decide how to operate among themselves, as leaders' meetings will be a point of vulnerability. Under torture a leader might identify other leaders which then opens the way for the exposure of other cells. Leaders might operate by knowing one or at the most two other leaders who then transmit information and decisions.

Modern technology, such as social media and Zoom meetings, can provide unexpected security as a person's location becomes hidden and they can use alternative identities. This has had negative consequences in society since people on social media can harm individuals they target whilst remaining anonymous, but it can also be turned to advantage in an underground situation[6].

The same principle should apply if there is more than one level of leadership, such as there might be in a large town.

I believe that this organisational structure allows the underground church the opportunity to function as described in earlier chapters. A cell might be in charge of praying for one or more streets. The first level of leadership would co-ordinate the prayer and activity of a district and so on until the town was covered. What I have described is basic unit (cell) security for an underground movement.

One difference between a military and an underground church movement

One key difference between a church cell and a wartime underground cell is that the cell will operate as a church for its people. Fellowship will be essential, whereas a wartime group can dispense with social interaction. Its activities can be governed entirely on a "need to know" basis – this creates greater security for the wartime cell.

Church cells will need to meet in people's homes, which will tend to limit their size, or they may choose to operate on Internet platforms, such as those we have become used to during the coronavirus pandemic. Their leader will need to assure them that they are operating along with other cells in their district or town and that when they pray their prayers are reaching God collectively; they will not be able to meet in large gatherings such as they could when the church operated openly.

A further risk to security

The second point at which security can be jeopardised is the need to evangelise. If the Church is to grow, then people must be told about Jesus. Here I believe it is essential to soak all evangelism in prayer. We can ask the Holy Spirit to point us to people who may respond to the gospel.

As a person or family's interest grows, they should be introduced very gradually to the cell, perhaps to the leader and certain other members before being invited to meet within the cell. The cell's prayer team can be seeking the Holy Spirit as to whether it is safe to proceed or whether contact should be quietly dropped.

There will be salvations where the Holy Spirit gives supernatural protection, but we must also remember that where God has permitted the authorities to suppress or restrict the church that he may intend for his people to go through persecution. That persecution can sometimes be the spark that triggers the spread of the gospel, as the public perceives how people are withstanding persecution, even to martyrdom[7].

The need to know one's Bible

One of the early signs that the Church may need to go underground is the state's attitude towards the Bible. In the twentieth century, Nazi Germany and the communist regimes sought to ban or even burn the Bibles. Possessing a Bible and certainly distributing a Bible could become a criminal offence. This makes it imperative to commit Bible verses to heart so that the underground Church and Christians in prison have the Word of God in their heart and on their lips.

The Tribulation

I have written a concise account of the Tribulation and the Antichrist in my book *The Return of Jesus Christ: the end or the beginning?* (Chapter 3) to which I refer readers.

All this talk of the underground Church may seem very "cloak and dagger" and it may be some while before it becomes relevant in the western democracies; but we are heading that way. More seriously, if the Church goes into the Tribulation (my book explains the alternative views), the talk of the underground Church and much more besides will become very relevant indeed. This is a time when God allows Satan full rein to persecute the believers in Jesus (*Revelation 12:11*) through the Antichrist and his false prophet.

The Church may well have been removed from earth by the time of the Tribulation (through the Rapture), but there will be many converts during this dreadful time, and they will need to be recruited to the underground Church.

The underground Church will face a further complication beyond operating in secret. The Bible forbids believers to take the mark of the Beast (Antichrist) – see *Revelation 13:16-18* and *14:9-11*. This will deny believers the opportunity to take part in ordinary commerce. Christian communities and cells will have to become self-sufficient, and they will have to do this under the cloak of secrecy.

Thus we can see that the idea of the underground Church, even in the western democracies, is not an improbable idea. It may become a necessary reality as the days become darker spiritually.

NOTES

1. See the bibliography for my book *The Return of Jesus Christ: the end or the beginning?*

2. The ten most repressive countries (in declining order) in 2021 were: North Korea, Afghanistan, Somalia, Libya, Pakistan, Eritrea, Yemen, Iran, Nigeria and India.

3. Google: Pope's support for same sex civil unions and same sex partners' right to have a family.

4. See my book *The Return of Jesus Christ: the end or the beginning? (Chapter 3)*.

5. Google: billionbibles.com/threeselfchurch

6. Of course, one has to be aware that the state will also be working on technology to overcome this problem of identifying anonymous users of social media and other communication platforms. I do find it astonishing that even today so many social media users can still remain anonymous.

7. *The Hiding Place* by Corrie ten Boom has some wonderful examples of God's protection in the face of adversity. Corrie and her sister Betsie did not escape the most terrible persecution. They were sent to prison and then to Ravensbruck concentration camp, but the Jews they were hiding in their home were not discovered, when they and the rest of their family were arrested *(Chapter 9 The Raid)*. On an earlier occasion when the Germans were rounding up young dutchmen for forced labour, they raided the ten Boom family home. Corrie's niece Cocky had been taught always to tell the truth; when asked by a German soldier whether she had brothers, she said "yes" and when asked where they were, she said: "under the table". They were in fact in a hideout under the kitchen floor hidden by a rug and trapdoor beneath the table. The German soldier threw back the tablecloth to find nothing and walked away furious, feeling he had been made to look foolish. Not everyone in the family agreed with this display of honesty! *(Chapter 7 Eusie)*. Perhaps the most striking example of God's protection was the way in which Corrie managed to secrete her precious Bible into Ravensbruck, despite the most

thorough searches. God had a purpose in this: once they were locked up in the dormitory each evening, they were able to hold Bible studies with many of the women prisoners *(Chapter 13 Ravensbruck).*

CHAPTER 17

SATAN FIGHTS BACK

I shall tackle this chapter in two stages. First, I will examine how Satan has sought to deflect the Church from its message, throughout church history. This is important because Satan is still using the same tactics in the Church today. Secondly, I will explain the ways in which Satan will seek to disrupt a church or group of churches once they have decided to wage war in the manner of this book.

CHURCH HISTORY

The Church may not understand that we are engaged in a battle, but Satan certainly does. He knows that he was defeated at the Cross (*Colossians 2:15*) and he therefore knows that once a person hears the message of salvation and this person wants to be born again that he cannot stop this from happening.

Throughout the last two millennia Satan has therefore resorted to a host of stratagems to prevent the Church from fulfilling its role. It is worth remembering that Satan succeeded in deflecting the Israelites from God's law and purposes. It is no surprise therefore to find that he has tried to do the same with the Church and that he has often succeeded. We shall now examine some of these stratagems.

1. Hiding
Satan has deceived large parts of the Church into believing that he and his kingdom are a figment of one's imagination. Talk of Satan in the Bible is a metaphor for evil, not the personification of evil. This is particularly true in modern times following the Enlightenment of the eighteenth and nineteenth centuries. Science was said to have superseded religious belief and people began to believe that miracles did not happen. Instead, whatever is not yet explained will one day be explained by science. It is

true that the discoveries of Science have been amazing, but that does not obviate the need for a creator! This deception is one reason why signs and wonders should accompany the preaching of the gospel. The reality of prophecy, speaking in tongues, healings and deliverance from demonic affliction have a powerful effect on people who may have thought that such things were fictitious or naturally explained[1].

This hidden aspect of Satan's activities means that many Christians may be unaware of the spiritual opposition when they witness to or pray for people. They may face a hard task without understanding why and this may discourage them.

2. Deflection

Quite early in Church history Satan encouraged the church to become a worldly structure pre-occupied with the trappings of power and one which eventually led to the persecution of true believers. This process began in the fourth century AD when Christianity became the State religion of the Roman Empire. This was formalised by the Emperor Theodosius I in 380 AD.

The Roman Catholic Church survived the collapse of the Western Roman Empire in 476 AD and itself became a powerful super-state in its own right, controlling the religious and political function of many European countries. This inevitably led to the persecution of true believers reaching a horrifying climax in the Spanish Inquisition beginning in 1478 AD and not finally ceasing until the early nineteenth century. It also led to the persecution of rabbinic Jews. They were forced to convert to Christianity on pain of death or expelled from Portugal and Spain in 1492 AD. This delusion was such that it was all done in the name of Christ!

3. Deception

During the long history of the Church Satan has persuaded it to adopt rituals that substitute for real salvation. This has deceived many churchgoers into thinking that merely attending church will get them to heaven. Infant baptism is another deception. It is good for parents to dedicate a child to God, but it should always be understood that each person, when old enough, has to make their own commitment to Christ.

4. Heresies

Heresies are another form of deception relating to the body of Christian belief. They began to occur early in the life of the Church. They are beliefs that depart from the canon of Old and New Testament scripture. In more recent times this has led to the so-called 'higher criticism' leading in turn to liberal theology[2]. It has led to the denial in some churches of the fundamental tenets of our faith. Examples would be: denial of Christ's divinity, denial of the virgin birth, denial of the reality of Christ's resurrection and denial of the existence of hell.

5. Cults

Heresies inspired by Satan have often appeared as Christian cults – sets of beliefs which give the impression that members are Christians while deflecting them from some fundamental biblical truth. These would include:

Jehovah's Witnesses
The Church of the Latter Day Saints (Mormons)
Christian Science
Christadelphians
Unitarians

They are all characterised by a human individual bringing some new revelation to add to Holy Scripture. The canon of scripture was finally agreed by the early Church Fathers in the fourth century AD and closed with the Book of Revelation. Scripture itself is very clear that nothing should be removed from it or added to it.

6. Disunity

Satan has successfully prevented churches from working together. Different denominations have emphasised different aspects of scripture and this is not in itself wrong. For example, the Baptists reintroduced full immersion baptism for adults, the Presbyterians emphasised church eldership while the Pentecostalists emphasised Pentecost and the baptism in the Holy Spirit. What Satan has succeeded in doing is to cause these denominations to look inwards instead of outwards and thus to prevent them from working with other churches in the common cause of spreading the gospel. As already mentioned in Chapter 12, I believe unity is a major key to defeating Satan and his kingdom. Despite this there are fine examples where churches agree to put theological differences aside and to work together.

7. Replacement Theology
Satan has fostered replacement theology, the view that Israel is no longer important in God's purposes for the Church or the world. This is decidedly unscriptural and has weakened the Church's effectiveness[3].

8. The Future
In recent years Satan has also succeeded in diminishing interest in what the Bible has to say about the end-times and Christ's return to earth. This has led to a loss of urgency over the need for the Church to declare its faith in salvation and the associated topic of judgement. The Church at large often avoids what it considers to be difficult subjects, which means that it does not provide a balanced view on sin, repentance, salvation and eternal judgement.

The impact of Satan's tactics in Church history
Consideration of the denials and deflections of belief all initiated or assisted by Satan's activities, should open our eyes to his ruthless tactics in deflecting the Church from its calling.

God has allowed this to happen, because we still have free will to follow or not to follow him, to obey or not to obey his commands. However, I am convinced that God intends to have the last word in relation to his Church as described in *Ephesians 4* and *5*. This is why I am convinced that the final wave of revival will see the Church manifest itself as a great army, ready to take on and pull down the satanic strongholds which prevent people coming to faith in Christ.

LOCAL WARFARE: SATAN FIGHTS BACK

We now consider the ways in which Satan may respond when he realises that a church or community of churches is serious about waging warfare and rescuing captives from the kingdom of darkness. The first point to remember is that Satan can only do what he does with God's permission, but within this context he knows his legal rights. The second point is that this is real warfare and God allows his soldiers to experience it. As in any human war there will be counter attacks, but provided we, as God's army, take all the defensive measures we can, these attacks will be to no avail. As we have seen in Chapter 11, we have the armour and the weaponry with which to defend ourselves and to take the offensive against the enemy.

Minimizing the counter attacks by Satan's demonic forces

It is a good idea for everyone who enlists in spiritual warfare against Satan's kingdom to make an inventory of all the things they might need to put right before the Lord. This would include unconfessed sin, unforgiveness, emotional problems and relationship issues. It would also include doing those things the Lord has been prompting them to do, however gently.[4]

Each person also needs to take stock of family and ancestral issues, particularly in relation to idolatry. If they know of parental or grandparental involvement in things like witchcraft or freemasonry, then it might be wise to seek counselling and ministry from Christians experienced in this field. One can then confess ancestors' involvement and even one's own involvement in a safe environment. The church may have leaders qualified for this, but if not then a person needs to seek the help of para-church organisations (see Glossary) such as Ellel Ministries, Prayer Warriors International or Sozo Ministries International.

If the Church is preparing for spiritual warfare, it may be a good idea **to address these issues collectively** for the leaders and the prayer teams. The church (or group of churches) might invite an appropriate para-church organisation to minister to the church. In my view this is a relevant and necessary preparation for taking on Satan. It is like a "cleansing of the stables"! We do not want the enemy to have any legal hold over either individuals or over prayer teams, and such preparations will neutralise any dominant curses or family iniquity. When this has been done it is important to remember to confess the scripture:

A curse without a cause will not alight.

(Proverbs 26:2 KJV)

Idolatry brings a curse, but once it is confessed and broken, Satan cannot restore it.

Satan's tactics

For many Christians, learning how to fend off Satan's attacks is as far as they get in this war between the two kingdoms. There is much teaching explaining how Christians need to stand firm against the enemy's attacks. In essence they should stand firm by resisting temptations and by speaking out the Word of God. Sadly there are also many failures! The Church and individual Christians so often appear to be on the defensive when it comes to Satan. This could be his first tactic – keeping people pre-occupied with health and behaviour problems, so they never get round to attacking him!

Before we examine Satan's tactics, I will assume that prospective warriors have been willing to seek serious help for their own problems and that these problems have, by and large, been resolved.

Individuals

Let us start with Satan's potential attacks on every individual Christian. How do we handle these? I mentioned earlier in the book that my wife and I decided that we should declare that we are putting on the armour of God each day, item by item, starting with the helmet of salvation. I thought about this for a long time, because some believers think this is ritualistic. We also ask God to protect us through the blood of Jesus. This has had an unexpected effect on me. It has activated the verse from the apostle Paul in which he says:

> Let this mind be in you which was also in Christ Jesus.
> *(Philippians 2:5 KJV)*

In short it has changed my mind-set. I now approach any attacks by the enemy with determination. I do not intend to allow them to land, let alone settle, and it works!

What does this mean in practice?

I immediately dismiss ungodly or unworthy thoughts. My attitude is that I will not have them. I recognise that these thoughts may be from my old nature (see *Romans 7*), but I also know that Satan can be waiting in the wings to exploit them. I thus apply the scripture given in *2 Corinthians:*

> . . . . *and take every thought captive to obey Christ.*
> *(2 Corinthians 10:5)*

When situations arise with people where there may be misunderstandings, I still need to be careful. It is a popular tactic with Satan to sow dissension between two people or between groups of people. It may be wise to apologise for something one has said, even when it may not seem that important.

Quoting from Scripture

We have learnt earlier in the book that the Word of God (the Bible) is the sword of the Spirit, so it makes sense to learn and proclaim verses from scripture[5]. These can be used in two ways: one may quote them back to God to stand on one of his promises (I believe God likes to hear us use scripture!), or one may use them to counter the attacks of the enemy or wage war against him. Many Christians are uncertain about which verses will prove most helpful, so I have printed a list in Appendix 4. One very useful verse to use against the enemy is the following from *Isaiah:*

> *No weapon formed against me shall succeed and I shall condemn every tongue that rises against me in judgment.*
> *(Isaiah 54:17)* [paraphrased]

Dreams and nightmares

Satan may attack through dreams and nightmares. I went through a phase of experiencing such attacks. When fully awake I would bind the enemy, declare I was washed clean in the blood of Jesus and tell the enemy to go. I eventually woke up praying this way before I was properly awake! Such dreams can be unpleasant and scary, but once one realises that it is a satanic attack, then it pays to be utterly ruthless in despatching the enemy.

Unexpected verbal attacks

Sometimes Satan will attack unexpectedly through another individual. The unexpectedness can be disturbing and bewildering. While it is right to challenge an untruth, it is very important to stay as calm as possible. Later one may have to forgive the individual (this is an **act**, not a feeling!) and pray for them. If the person is an unbeliever, then pray for their salvation (Satan will not like this). If the attack is really unpleasant then it may be wise to seek prayer within one's church. Such unexpected verbal attacks can come when one is about to start an important new adventure in one's Christian life. We need to remember too that God may allow such an attack, because he wants to use it to teach us some truth.

Sickness

Sicknessis a tactic that may be used by the enemy to disrupt an important Christian work, especially one that targets a specific satanic stronghold. My own view, one that some Christian leaders may disagree with, is that this is only possible if there is a chink in one's spiritual armour. This is why it is so important for Christian warriors to resolve issues in their lives before engaging in warfare.

Healing

Healing - the reverse of sickness – is part of our redemption in Christ. We should be saved, healed and delivered. This is what Jesus did while on earth: Jesus healed and delivered and those who believed in him were saved. Matthew says:

> *That evening they brought to him many who were oppressed by demons, and he cast out the spirits with a word and healed all who were sick. This was to fulfill what was spoken by the prophet Isaiah: "He took our illnesses and bore our diseases."*
> *(Matthew 8:16-17)*

I acknowledge that God himself uses sickness to discipline people or to test them in both the Old and New Testaments. He may choose to use Satan as his agent of sickness, as we see very clearly in the story of Job. However, this is about our relationship with God. If we have been called to be a warrior in the warfare against Satan, then I do not think God wants us sick, unless there is an opening in our spiritual armour.[6]

Church leaders and prayer team leaders

Satan's major tactic here will be to divide and rule. He will try to stop the warfare getting off the ground by lack of enthusiasm and by disagreement over the approach. Such attacks will be motivated by demons and the leaders will need to pray against and to bind the enemy forces involved.

A follow-up tactic will be to raise up opposition in the local community. Handling this will need wisdom and prayer since the mission must continue. Both the warfare and the back-up teams can be involved in praying against the opposition. The teams should ask God to turn this opposition to their advantage. The Old Testament has many examples of how the Lord sowed confusion in the ranks of Israel's enemies. God wants us to wage war, but he also wants us to lean on him – the battle against Satan is still God's battle.

Satan will seek to expose any unrighteousness in the churches, especially among the leaders – another reason for them to get right with God in every respect. Church leaders in particular need to be aware that Satan himself uses prayer to damage Christians. It is known that he seeks to attack Christian marriages and break them up through the 'prayers' and curses of witches and Satanists. Marriage is a covenant and especially sacred to God, so he will not let this succeed without just cause, but Satan will try to exploit any sin or weakness in a leader's marriage.

Simon, Simon, Satan has demanded to have you . . .

I want to finish this chapter on a more personal note. In a book like this where the two kingdoms of righteousness and evil are counterposed so directly, it is easy to forget that God in his infinite wisdom has chosen to use his enemy Satan in the process of fashioning a people (believers) for himself. God is going to close down Satan and his rebellious kingdom of fallen angels and demons at some time in the future. Meanwhile he may choose to use Satan to help fashion us in the image of his son Jesus.

This is a strange fact, but it is an undeniable truth of scripture. As we have already seen, Satan has retained some authority which the scripture makes clear must be respected by other angelic beings (*Jude 9*). Satan still has the right to appear before God, and furthermore he can demand to test those who confess Christ. We saw in the early chapters of Job how God gave Satan permission to wreak havoc in Job's life. Job was a righteous man and God knew that he would come through the testing, damaged, but intact. He held onto his faith in God through terrible suffering, completely unaware of what was going on in the spiritual realm. Job experienced what is sometimes described as a **wilderness experience** and these can be of long duration. The Lord may seem to have disappeared from one's life! Nevertheless, it is a time of testing ordained by God and through which we have to pass. It cannot be bypassed.

Turning to the New Testament we have the famous passage in Luke:

> *Simon, Simon, behold, Satan [has] demanded to have you, that he might sift you like wheat, but I [Jesus] have prayed for you that your faith may not fail.*
>
> *(Luke 22:31)*

Satan had the right to demand that he be allowed to test Simon Peter. What can happen to Peter can also happen to other believers. I believe Satan makes good use of this right of testing when God calls believers to a particular work. It is likely too, that God will warn us with this very same scripture that Jesus spoke to Peter.

I would say to every reader who receives this warning either directly from scripture or in some other way; **consider this a badge of honour from God!** The journey will not be easy – "sifting like wheat' suggests a thorough going over, but God is allowing this to prepare you for the work to which he has called you. The journey may be long or short, and the testing will be tough; Satan will target our particular weakness or weaknesses. What is required of us is to hold fast to God and to his Word. Offensive weapons like binding and loosing will not be of help here. We are the ones on the anvil or potter's wheel with God's full agreement, but if we hold fast to our faith during this time, the Lord promises a wonderful outcome:

Behold, I have refined you, but not as silver, I have tried you in the furnace of affliction.

(Isaiah 48:10)

But he knows the way that I take; when he has tried me, I shall come forth as gold. My foot has held fast to his steps; I have kept his way and not turned aside. I have not departed from the commandments of his lips; I have treasured in my bosom the words of his mouth.

(Job 23:10-12 RSV)

NOTES

1. The evidence of supernatural manifestations by the Holy Spirit and the fulfilment of biblical prophecy were important in the author's own coming to faith in Christ.

2. **Higher Criticism** came to its peak towards the end of the nineteenth century and the early twentieth century. It investigates the origins of ancient texts, such as the Bible, in order to understand the meaning behind the text, instead of accepting the texts at face value. It assumes a secular perspective and thus automatically denies the supernatural inspiration of scripture. The method is intent on finding natural explanations for events which are described as supernatural in the scriptures. This inevitably led to liberal theological views which deny the virgin birth of Christ and his supernatural resurrection.

3. For a fuller explanation of replacement theology and the harm it is doing to the Church, see the author's book: *Has God Really finished with Israel?* (details in the Bibliography)

4. The author owns up to such a prompting by God: we used to live in a house with a porch with an unprotected drop of one foot between pillar and wall on one side of this porch. My wife had expressed concern about this over the years which regrettably I had never taken on board, partly through not being sure how to resolve it and partly through feeling it was safe through warning parents of children who visited the house. A few years ago, however, an older member of one of our prayer groups pointed out the danger and it struck me that this was exactly the sort of situation the enemy could exploit. Accepting this might be a prompt from God and with apologies to my wife, I moved to block the problem by having a gate installed!

5. When using or proclaiming scriptures one does not have to remember the exact wording; after all the many translations of the Bible vary in their precise wording.

6. The subject of healing is huge and often controversial – it deserves a book to itself and many have been written! This author does believe that healing should be a natural part of our redemption in Christ. However, I recognise that there are several reasons why people do not get healed. One is that they may need healing in their spirit and soul before this healing manifests itself in their bodies. This is

why the "total health" approach of organisations such as Ellel and Sozo Ministries International is so important. Another, possibly very significant reason why people do not get healed is that the Church rejected healing and deliverance in the early centuries of its existence. It may need a wholesale re-acceptance by the Church at large, before healing is restored to its rightful place in Church ministry (see *The Healing Reawakening by Francis MacNutt*).

CHAPTER 18

THE FRUITS OF VICTORY

Jesus uses a powerful agricultural metaphor about salvation and entering the kingdom of God. He describes the human souls awaiting salvation as a harvest field, a metaphor repeated with variations in each of the four gospels (*Matthew 9:37; Luke 10:2; Mark 4:6* and *John 4:35*). He tells the disciples that the harvest is ready and furthermore that the labourers are few. He distinguishes between the sower and the reaper (*John 4:37*). The sower will have prayed and waged spiritual warfare on behalf of the lost, while the reaper, a friend, pastor or evangelist will bring them to the prayer of repentance. The sower and the reaper may indeed be the same person.

> *The harvest is plentiful, but the labourers few, therefore pray earnestly to the Lord of the harvest to send out labourers into his harvest.*
>
> (*Matthew 9:37-38*)

> *Do you not say: "There are yet four months, then comes the harvest? Look, I tell you, lift up your eyes, and see that the fields are white for harvest."*
>
> (*John 4:35*)

The Church as an army

In this book I have argued that the Church can best achieve this harvest when it is organised as an army. In many places in the world a harvest of souls for the kingdom is already being reaped. In other places the strongholds of the enemy are such that the harvest is not ready. The seed may not even have been sown. The soil needs to be tilled, sown and watered before the corn can start to grow.

As the world gets darker spiritually, the opposition to the things of God becomes stronger. I believe that God wants his Church to become an army which shines its light into the darkness. I believe he wants to manifest his glory through his Church before the final darkness of this age arrives. I also believe that he will use this time to sift the Church for those who would embrace disciplined spiritual warfare from those who would shrink back.

There will be an end-times harvest and maybe we are entering that time. Several prophetic voices have had a vision for such a harvest.

What I have done in this book is to provide guidelines as to how the Church in general might go about this. **I have emphasised that the chapters on warfare are not meant to be a template for action.** Circumstances and personalities differ from place to place, and leaders must choose the best way in their locality to become an army for the Lord.

Modern-day revivals

In this last chapter I do have to address the issue of why there is so much revival in certain parts of the world, if the Church is not consciously waging spiritual warfare. My short answer is that the Church has been waging warfare, even if it has not been conscious of it. Believers have worshipped, they have prayed, they have fasted, they have repented and **perhaps most important of all they have worked together with other churches**. That covers a significant part of the weapons of warfare mentioned in Chapter 11. Nevertheless, I think the issue requires further explanation.

I will illustrate this by reference to what has happened in Latin America. This is not to diminish the revivals that have also happened in many other countries in Africa, Asia and elsewhere. Over the last thirty years, revival has been sweeping across parts of Latin America with many thousands of people entering the kingdom of God.

Colombia
Colombia is one such country. Thirty years ago, it was the drugs capital of the world. The government was at war with Marxist guerrillas and much of society was controlled by cocaine cartels. It was considered one of the most dangerous countries on earth. Today it is a great deal safer. The government has negotiated peace with Marxists and the cartels have either been defeated or

moved elsewhere. The country is in much better shape socially and economically and in terms of security. It would be a mistake though to assume that all is well. Satan and his forces have had to retreat, but they are still around, particularly in the countryside. What is different is that there are thousands of Christian converts who pray for the nation.

Pastor Ricardo and Patricia Rodriguez[1] sought the Lord 25 years ago for his presence and the presence of the Holy Spirit. Eventually this led to the huge revival seen in Bogota, Medellin and other towns in Colombia. The people prayed against the principalities and powers governing the drug cartels and they prayed for unity among the churches. A pivotal moment occurred in 1995 when 25,000 believers gathered in the civic auditorium in Bogota. This led to the fall of the first drug baron, and the collapse of the cocaine cartels, but it came at a cost. The devil hit back, and an assassin was despatched to kill the Bolivian preacher Julio Ruibal (known as "the apostle of the Andes"). His martyrdom put the seal on this revival.

Carlos Annacondia

I have been particularly impressed to read about Carlos Annacondia[2] from Argentina, a very humble evangelist now in his seventies who is still seeing thousands come to Christ across Latin American countries. Much fervent prayer precedes each of his rallies and he frequently starts each meeting by challenging demonic spirits to make themselves known. Demonic manifestation follows, with assistants on hand to lead people to an adjacent tent where they can receive deliverance ministry. This immediately clears the atmosphere for the Holy Spirit to work in the main meeting.

What strikes me about this practice is that if other preachers operated in the same way, it might avoid the excesses and spiritual mixture seen in some charismatic outreaches. This "mixture" has caused many believers to recoil as they feel instinctively that many manifestations are not those of the Holy Spirit.

It gladdens the heart to see such revival, but we cannot assume that the countries themselves will become part of the kingdom of God. Satan is still the ruler of this world (*1 John 5:19*) and still waiting to return after his retreat. So long as Christians continue to pray, he will be held back. However, the real fruit of victory from these revivals is not the temporary displacement of satanic forces, **but the transferring of thousands of people from Satan's kingdom**

of darkness to God's kingdom of light. They now have a place in eternity with God.

Is revival solely a sovereign work of God?

I live in a country (the United Kingdom) which is in a state of moral decay. It has not seen the sort of revival we are seeing in Latin America, Africa and China in a very long time. In fact, preachers have given up talking about revival. Nevertheless, many devout Christians over many years have prayed for such a revival and believe that Britain will play a significant part in the last great end-times revival. Meanwhile, the Church has declined in Britain and in many denominations it has departed from sound biblical principles by embracing the beliefs and the ways of the world.

The question arises: is revival solely a sovereign move of God or is it something that happens in partnership between God and his Church? I believe the timing of revival is entirely in God's hands. However, I believe the scriptures, both Old and New Testaments, point to a partnership between God and his people. He led, but also partnered with Israel in its very real warfare with its surrounding enemies and he also partners with the Church to bring people into his kingdom. He has given a very great responsibility to the Church. Both at the end of Matthew and Marks' gospels Jesus tells the disciples to go out and make disciples of all nations while he (from heaven) works with them. This verse speaks of partnership:

> *And they went out and preached everywhere while the Lord worked with them and confirmed the message by accompanying signs.*
>
> *(Mark 16:20)*

Returning to revivals presently occurring, I very much doubt that they would have happened independently of Christians praying in many countries, both those where the revival is occurring and also in other countries. Christians will be aware of how God puts countries on people's hearts. I can think of people who have been called to pray for Japan, Poland and Israel in my former church. This may lead to the sending of missionaries to such countries[3]. Every time a person or group of people is called in this way, they may have waged spiritual warfare without realising it.

Does the Church really need to be an army?

If the above is true, is what I am proposing really necessary? Does God really need us to be an army along the lines I have suggested? I believe the answer is "yes" for several reasons:

1. My principal reason is that the Church consciously functioning as a spiritual army, under the direction of the Holy Spirit, will be organised and disciplined. Much church activity is fragmented or disjointed often with little to show for it. In a country like Britain many people have sought the Lord over many years only to find the Church at large shrinking and coming under false doctrine. **I have stressed the importance of working together throughout this book and I believe that this alone would bear fruit.** However, working as a disciplined and a united force would bring much more fruit. The enemy would be confronted by a Church that had a mission, understood this mission and knew how to use its weapons to fulfil this mission.

2. Some parts of the world are not as ready for harvesting as others. The strongholds of the enemy are such that the harvest is nowhere near ready. The corn still needs to grow and a disciplined army of the Lord can help to bring this about.

3. As the world gets darker spiritually the opposition to the things of God becomes stronger. The Church **recognising itself as an army** will be in a better place to oppose Satan than it has been in the past.

4. I believe, as we approach the end-times and the expected last wave of revival, that God wants and intends to display his glory through his Church to a dying world. This Church will manifest the full gospel: salvation, healing, deliverance and the gifts of the Holy Spirit will be fully on display. No more debates over whether certain things belonged only to the first century Church. The debates will be settled by those things happening. We shall see the greater works of which Jesus spoke. Let us step back and think about this:

*Truly, truly, I say to you, whoever believes in me will also do the works that I do; and **greater works than these will he do**, because I am going to the Father.*

(John 14:12) [emphasis added]

Greater works? I should be happy to do what Jesus did, but the Bible promises greater works![4]

Victorious warriors

The reader will not find many references in contemporary literature to the Church as an army, or to organised opposition to Satan. There is much written about taking on the enemy at an individual level and even to setting places free from demonic control. This is essentially **defensive ministry**. This book, however, is about **offensive ministry**. By an army I mean the Church being organised, principally at the local level, to take on the enemy and break down his strongholds.

Nevertheless, many Christian leaders do recognise this role for the Church, even though they may not necessarily refer to it as an army. Francis Frangipane writes with real experience of spiritual warfare and the need to unite when praying for one's city. I was especially influenced by his book *The Three Battlegrounds*[6].

A very influential book was written by John Dawson in 1989 (updated 2001) entitled *Taking our Cities for God*[7]. He has much to say on the subject of spiritual warfare, but his central illustration concerns the 1984 Olympic Games in Los Angeles.

I shall close this chapter of my book with a description of what happened. **To me it exactly encapsulates the Church in action as an army**. He describes the spiritual battle over his home city of Los Angeles in the run-up to the Olympics in the summer of 1984.

Los Angeles – 1984 Summer Olympics

Los Angeles was a sin city with an oppressive spiritual atmosphere for believers. In 1983 John and other leaders knew that the world's attention would be on Los Angeles with many thousands of foreign visitors coming to the city for the Olympic Games the following summer. This would be a once in a lifetime opportunity for the Church. Eventually over 1600 churches united in an active coalition.

Ten different sub-committees were dedicated to various forms of evangelism, but everyone came together to pray.

Following the conception of the outreach, over 200 pastors and leaders met for three days of prayer. Prayer networks were activated across the nation and around the world. One group of praying women purchased detailed city maps and spent months praying over the inhabitants of every street. Congregations prayed individually and at citywide events. An international prayer conference in South Korea with over 300,000 attendees prayed for the Los Angeles Olympics. The media carried interviews and articles calling for prayer for a great harvest. Pastors began to meet monthly for prayer at the Olympic Village site.

When the outreach finally began, the spiritual atmosphere of the city had totally changed. Harvest time had come. The churches came together to organise a huge interactive praise gathering in a Los Angeles stadium. Christians from nearly every church in the city were joined by believers from over 30 countries to reach a crowd of 16,000. It was a night devoted to praise and worship to the Lord. That night the enemy was defeated. The days following the outreach saw a huge harvest of souls for the kingdom.

Teams reported more than 1,000 people a day coming to Jesus. It was a time of Holy Spirit anointing and divine appointments. Crime diminished and according to the city coroner there were no murders in Los Angeles during the two weeks of the Olympics. People became cheerful and friendly. Even the summer traffic jams and air pollution failed to materialise.

John closes his account with these words:

"During the summer of 1984 Christians in Los Angeles briefly experienced a city free from spiritual oppression."

The word **'briefly'** is significant. This spiritual warfare is on-going. The moment it relaxes, Satan comes back. What really matters, however, is that several thousand people have been transferred from Satan's kingdom into God's kingdom. **That is the purpose of our warfare**.

The lesson John Dawson draws from this outreach is as follows:

> *"The most lasting legacy of this outreach and perhaps God's true objective was the uniting of scattered, pre-occupied spiritual leaders into **a co-ordinated army** with a common set of goals. In this unity we found that we had new power to hold back the forces of darkness. We experienced great success in evangelism. We learned to discern the territorial spirits operating over a city and to break their yoke through spiritual warfare."*[8]

(emphasis added)

To me this is a fine example of the Church in action as an army. Let us repeat it in Britain and elsewhere where society is in moral decay.

Conclusion

I believe the Church, if it is willing to return to its roots and to hear from God, has a wonderful future in bringing people into the kingdom of God and saving them from a lost eternity.

NOTES

1. Charisma Magazine – Sustained Revival Ignites Holy Ghost Transformation in Latin America (Google the article).

2. Premier Christianity – Carlos Annacondia: The evangelist at the forefront of revival (Google).

3. It is worth mentioning that the work of missionaries in Israel is sensitive because of the opposition of Orthodox Jews to the gospel.

4. My observation is not to deny that amazing miracles already happen in many revival meetings going on today and some may already constitute 'greater works'.

5. *The Three Battlegrounds. Part Three: The Battleground in the Heavenly Places* P101.

6. *Taking our Cities for God* P46-48 and 130.

7. Ibid, P48.

APPENDICES

APPENDICES

Appendix 1

What is the Church?

The Church is the worldwide body of believers in Jesus Christ as Saviour and Lord. This will include those already in heaven through death and those still alive on earth. It comprises millions of souls. (Reference to the worldwide Church is usually made with a capital 'C' to contrast it with the local church.)

Most individuals are concerned with that part of the Church they happen to belong to or have chosen to do so. If their local church supports missionaries in other countries, then they will have some understanding of the extent of the worldwide Church or Body of Christ.

Thus, for most believers their local church is what matters to them. It is where they worship God, pray, have Bible study, make friends and serve in different ways.

The Local Church

However, it is my firm belief that when God looks down on a city, town or rural area, he sees one local church. The denominations which over the ages have become so important to us, are much less important to him. I firmly believe that he wants to see these local churches co-operating in what they do for the kingdom – too often this is not the case.

In New Testament times it is quite possible that there were several local churches in the city of Corinth, but when Paul wrote his letters to the Corinthian church he addressed them as one part of the Body of Christ.

One other aspect of the Church

There is a further consideration to bear in mind: the Church also contains people who, for whatever reason, have not understood or been taught that God wants them to have a personal relationship with him through Jesus Christ; in other words, to repent and be born-again. They may feel that attending church and leading good moral lives is enough to become a Christian. This is particularly true of the larger denominations where the true gospel of salvation through Jesus Christ may not be preached, or attending church may be a matter of family tradition.

For believers who do understand what it means to have a personal relationship with Jesus, it is necessary to be sensitive to such members of the Church, but also legitimate to explain the gospel and to pray for them to come into this understanding.

APPENDIX 2

SOUND DOCTRINE AND FAITH

It would be wonderful to see as many churches as possible working together as an army. However, I recognise that there needs to be a commonality in the fundamentals of their faith. Churches with a liberal theology are most unlikely to want to join in such warfare. We are therefore talking about evangelical/charismatic churches and I think it is most important that we do not exclude churches on anything other than the fundamental tenets of the faith.

Here are my suggestions, but leaders may want to tweak them, and it will be a matter for each set of local churches to decide. I think churches will need to be in agreement on the following points:

1. There is one God who exists as three Persons: Father, Son and Holy Spirit.

2. God is omnipotent (all powerful), omnipresent (exists everywhere) and omniscient (sees everything).

3. The Bible, both the Old and New Testaments, is the inspired word of God.

4. God the Son was conceived by the Holy Spirit and born of the Virgin Mary, to grow up as the God-Man Jesus Christ. Christ was and is divine.

5. Jesus lived a sinless life on earth and suffered a substitutionary atoning death on the Cross, so that sinful human beings could be set free to be reconciled to God.

6. Jesus experienced a miraculous bodily resurrection from the grave and now dwells in heaven. While in heaven his Church, empowered by the Holy Spirit, represents him here on earth.

7. Salvation is by faith and not by works, though works are important in the Christian life.

8. Salvation through faith in the atoning work of Christ, is the only way to God.

9. There is a spiritual kingdom of darkness headed by Satan which is in opposition to the kingdom of God.

APPENDIX 3

THE BIBLE – HOW TO APPROACH AND UNDERSTAND IT

In my first two books I devoted a whole chapter to the subject of how to read the Bible with its use of allegory and metaphor. This time round I am just going to give a brief resume.

Essential Things

There are two essential things to understand when reading the Bible. First, it is the inspired Word of God to humanity. God has spoken directly through Jesus and the prophets, and he has caused others to write down what he wants humanity to hear. Secondly, the Old and New Testaments form a seamless whole. There is no discontinuity. The Old Testament ushers in the New; a fact established by the frequent quotations from the Old Testament by Jesus himself and all the New Testament writers.

The Origin of the Scriptures

The early Church lived by the Old Testament. There was no written New Testament. The Jewish Tanach (The Church's Old Testament) represented the written texts for the early Church. The message of salvation through Jesus was transmitted verbally for many years after his death and resurrection. Gradually a collection of letters and writings were built up to define doctrine and church practice. These were inspired by the Holy Spirit and eventually collected into what became the New Testament canon. In the early years of the Church, God allowed some fluidity as to what was considered canon. For example, the letter to the Hebrews was at first excluded from the canon. Today, with its pivotal role in defining the various God-given covenants, believers would find this astonishing; it seems such an essential document.

There are many books outside the canon of Protestant scripture; some of these constitute the Apocrypha which the Catholic Church considers to be part of the canon. Some of these, such as Maccabees I and II, serve as valuable historical documents.

The Role of the Holy Spirit

Another test as to the authority of scripture is whether the Holy Spirit brings it alive for the reader. To the non-believer this sounds highly subjective, but to the believer it is very meaningful. I find some of the apocryphal books interesting, and they may contain biblical truths, but they never come alive in the way that the Old and New Testament canon does. In short, they cannot be relied on as the Word of God.

There is simply no place for doubting the truth of scripture or choosing those parts which one approves of, while dismissing the parts one does not like. This is where liberal theology has gone so wrong and led Christians into doctrinal error.

Scripture is the inspired, complete Word of God for the benefit of humanity.

APPENDIX 4

USEFUL SCRIPTURES IN THE WARFARE WITH SATAN

These scriptures are provided as a ready reference of suitable material to use in spiritual warfare. Some can be used directly in prayer to God to remind him of what he has promised in his Word. Others have been slightly paraphrased so that they can be spoken or proclaimed directly to the enemy. For example, in some verses I have changed the second person 'you' to 'I' or 'we' so that the prayer warrior can appropriate them directly to his or her situation. I have quoted the verses from different versions of the Bible without indicating which version. Each reader may wish to look up the verse and see if they prefer a different version. Satan and his forces will be well aware of the scriptures and understand their meaning or intent.

Verses suitable for warfare

For the word of God is living and powerful, and   Hebrews 4:12
sharper than any two-edged sword, piercing even
to the division of soul and spirit, and of joints and
marrow, and is a discerner of the thoughts and
intents of the heart.

No weapon formed against me shall succeed,   Isaiah 54:17
And every tongue which rises against me in
judgment, I shall condemn. This is the heritage of
the servants of the Lord.

A curse without cause shall not alight.   Proverbs 26.2

For God has not given us a spirit of fear, but of power and of love and of a sound mind.	2 Timothy 1:7
The God of peace will soon crush Satan under our (my) feet.	Romans 16:20
The Lord has commanded me. I am strong and of good courage; I am not afraid, nor dismayed, for the Lord my God is with me wherever I go.	Joshua 1:9
I am (we are) strong in the Lord and in the strength of his might.	Ephesians 6:10
Believers have conquered Satan by the blood of the Lamb and by the word of their testimony, for they loved not their lives even unto death.	Revelation 12:11
Can the prey be taken from the mighty, or the captives of a tyrant be rescued? Surely, thus says the Lord: "Even the captives of the mighty shall be taken, and the prey of the tyrant be rescued, for I will contend with those who contend with you."	Isaiah 49:24-25
For the weapons of our warfare are not worldly but have divine power to destroy strongholds. We destroy arguments and every proud obstacle to the knowledge of God, and take every thought captive to obey Christ,	2 Corinthians 10:4-5
No one can enter a strong man's house and plunder his goods, unless he first binds the strong man. And then **we** can plunder his house.	Mark 3:27
What do you (*the enemy*) conspire against the Lord? He will make an utter end of it. Affliction will not rise up a second time.	Nahum 1:9

Righteousness exalts a nation, but sin is a reproach to any people.	Proverbs 14:34

Christ's Authority

Having disarmed principalities and powers, he made a public example of them, triumphing over them through it (the Cross).	Colossians 2.15
God the Father has seated Jesus at His right hand in the heavenly places, far above all principality and power and might and dominion, and every name that is named, not only in this age, but also in the age to come.	Ephesians 1:20-21
God the Father has put all things under his feet, and has given Jesus to be head over all things to the church.	Ephesians 1:22
For I am persuaded that neither death nor life, nor angels nor principalities nor powers, . . . nor any other created thing, shall be able to separate us from the love of God which is in Christ Jesus our Lord.	Romans 8:38-39
The Lord said: So shall my word be that goes forth from my mouth; it shall not return to me empty, but it shall accomplish that which I purpose, and prosper in the thing for which I sent it.	Isaiah 55:11

Our Authority and our Place in Christ

For this purpose the Son of God was manifested, that He might destroy the works of the devil.	1 John 3:8

Jesus said: If you abide in me, and my words abide in you, ask whatever you will, and it shall be done for you. John 15:7

We are of God, and have overcome them; for he who is in us is greater than he who is in the world. 1 John 4:4

We believe there is one God; we do well. Even the demons believe--and shudder. James 2:19

Jesus said: Behold, I give you the authority to trample on serpents and scorpions, and over all the power of the enemy, and nothing shall by any means hurt you. Luke 10:19

Jesus said: "I will give you the keys of the kingdom of heaven, and whatever you bind on earth will be bound in heaven, and whatever you loose on earth will be loosed in heaven". Matthew 16:19

The Spirit of the Lord is upon me (Jesus), because the Father has anointed me to preach the gospel to the poor; He has sent me to heal the brokenhearted, to proclaim liberty to the captives and recovery of sight to the blind, to set at liberty those who are oppressed. Luke 4:18

I have been crucified with Christ; it is no longer I who live, but Christ who lives in me; and the life I now live in the flesh I live by faith in the Son of God, who loved me and gave himself for me. Galatians 2:20

We destroy arguments and every proud obstacle to the knowledge of God, and take every thought captive to obey Christ. 2 Corinthians 10:5

The Blood of Christ

If we walk in the light as he is in the light . . . the blood of Jesus Christ his Son cleanses us from all sin. **1 John 1:7**

We have been ransomed . . . . with the precious blood of Christ. **1 Peter 1:18-20**

Repentance

If My people who are called by My name will humble themselves, and pray and seek My face, and turn from their wicked ways, then I will hear from heaven, and will forgive their sin and heal their land. **2 Chronicles 7:14**

While I (Daniel) was speaking and praying, confessing my sin and the sin of my people Israel, and presenting my plea before the Lord my God for the holy hill of my God. **Daniel 9:20**

The Israelites separated themselves from all foreigners, and stood and confessed their sins and the iniquities of their fathers. **Nehemiah 9:2**

Protection

God is faithful, and he will not let me be tempted beyond my strength, but with the temptation will also provide the way of escape, that I may be able to endure it. **1 Corinthians 10:13**

I will not fear the terror of the night, nor the arrow that flies by day. **Psalm 91:5**

I sought the Lord, and he answered me, and delivered me from all my fears. Psalm 34:4

You (the Lord) keep me in perfect peace whose mind is stayed on you, because I trust in you. Isaiah 26:3

The blessing of the Lord makes rich, and he adds no sorrow with it. Proverbs 10:22

I trust in the Lord with all my heart, and lean not to my own understanding; in all my ways I acknowledge him, and he shall direct my paths. Proverbs 3:5-6

For I know the plans I have for you, declares the Lord, plans for good and not for evil, to give you a future and a hope. Jeremiah 29:11

The name of the Lord is a strong tower; the righteous man runs into it and is safe. Proverbs 18:10

For I have not received the spirit of slavery to fall back into fear, but I have received the spirit of sonship. When I cry, "Abba! Father!" Romans 8:15

The Son has made me free, so I am free indeed. John 8:36

Yet I will rejoice in the Lord, I will joy in the God of my salvation. God the Lord is my strength, Habakkuk 3:18-19

When going through a testing time

I will forget my misery; I will remember it as waters that have passed away. Job 11:16

I count it all joy, my brethren, when I meet   James 1:2-3
various trials, for I know that the testing of my
faith produces steadfastness.

Behold, I (the Lord) have refined you, but not as   Isaiah 48:10
silver; I have tested you in the furnace of affliction.

But he knows the way that I take; when he has   Job 23:10-12
tried me, I shall come forth as gold.

BREXIT AND THE EUROPEAN UNION

I have mentioned Brexit – the United Kingdom's referendum vote to leave the European Union in 2016 – several times in the text, and Christian readers, both in Britain and elsewhere, may be wondering why this is important.

The short answer is that Britain was misled in the 1975 referendum into confirming entry into what was then a common market in goods[1] and not the economic and political union of countries it has now become, run by an unelected Commission, only partly accountable to elected representatives and to heads of government. The drive to make this a fully integrated United States of Europe continues.

A Brief History

Once the Romans left the British Isles in AD 410, Britain has always succeeded in maintaining its independence from Europe. Although Catholic until the time of the Reformation it remained outside the Holy Roman Empire[2] which ran from AD 800 until its final dissolution at the time of Napoleon in 1806. Britain avoided being annexed to the European empire of Napoleon and it successfully defeated Hitler's attempts in the Second World War to incorporate it in a greater Europe under German domination. 1973 was the first time in over 1500 years that Britain voluntarily began to surrender its sovereignty to Europe.

The Spiritual Reason

The longer answer as to why it is important to leave the European Union (EU) is a spiritual one. Satan has been drawing European countries together in an empire which is likely to become the revived Roman Empire of which Daniel the prophet speaks (*Daniel 9-11*) and through which the Antichrist will become manifest. There is plenty of evidence to demonstrate that the European Union has become an increasingly godless organisation and is under the control of a satanic principality from which the United Kingdom needs to escape.

It is right to recognise that in human terms the old European Economic Community (Common Market) was initiated by politicians and statesmen who sought a way out of the devastating world wars which had plagued Europe in the first half of the twentieth century. It is said that at the founding of the EEC the prime ministers of Germany, France and Italy actually prayed together, and its early days (1950s/60s) envisaged an organisation based on Judaeo-Christian principles. Today, however, things are very different.

Europe now has a common currency (the Euro), and leaders are calling for a United States of Europe with the unelected Commission as its government. There is evidence too that they are delineating regions of Europe so as to break down national borders and thus strip countries of their national identity. These regions are known as 'Interreg". The idea is sold to the public as creating common geographical areas for infrastructure development and other community initiatives. The Bible speaks of a confederacy of ten kingdoms arising in the last days, from which the Antichrist will appear (*Daniel 7*). The following suggestion is supposition, but if the EU continues on the road to a super-state, then the supplanting of its current 28 countries with ten administrative kingdoms could be the explanation of Daniel's prophecy[3].

This information alone should be enough to want an individual nation such as Britain to leave and to re-establish its sovereignty over its affairs. However, the satanic origin and control of this empire makes it essential for Britain to come out from under this control.

Let us look at the evidence:

1. God did not intend the human race to live in empires. The nation-state was his intention – not a collection of states in empires where the leader and ruling class amass dictatorial power (*Job 12:23; Acts 17:26*).

2. Early in human history man sought power and independence from God as illustrated by Nimrod and the Tower of Babel (*Genesis 10-11*). God dealt swiftly with this rebellion by multiplying human languages, so people had to stay within their language group and were subsequently dispersed across the world to become tribes and later nation-states.

3. The European Union has followed the same path as Nimrod and the first Babylonians and can expect God's judgement. God has been deliberately excluded from the European Constitution (2004). The updated constitution brings together the many treaties on which the EU is based including the Lisbon Treaty (2007). The preamble to its constitution refers to:

   > *Drawing inspiration from the cultural, religious and **humanist** inheritance of Europe, from which have developed the universal values of the inviolable and inalienable rights of the human person, freedom, democracy, equality and the rule of law.*
   >
   > [emphasis added]

   The decision to exclude mention of God was taken, despite protest, by a drafting convention which considered a paper entitled "*Let's leave God out of this*" by Josep Borrell, a Spanish member of the convention. Valery Giscard d'Estaing, the convention's chairman was committed to a humanist approach to the constitution of the EU.

   There is also a view that the highly unusual looking EU Parliament building in Strasbourg was erected in the image of the Tower of Babel as depicted in the famous painting by Pieter Brueghel of 1563. However, we cannot be entirely sure about this[4].

4. The European Union uses the image of "*a woman riding a beast*". This is found on its two-Euro coin and on certain documents. It is also appears as a painting, a mural and a sculpture in Brussels and Strasbourg. One might wonder why the European Union should want to use this image which encapsulates a story from Greek mythology[5], but many Christians will see a prophetic

significance to a passage in Revelation:

> *And I saw a woman sitting on a scarlet beast that was full of blasphemous names, and it had seven heads and ten horns. The woman was arrayed in scarlet and purple, and adorned with gold and jewels and pearls, holding in her hand a golden cup full of abominations and the impurities of her sexual immorality. And on her forehead was written a name of mystery: Babylon the great, mother of prostitutes and of earth's abominations. And I saw the woman drunk with the blood of the saints, the blood of the martyrs of Jesus.*
> *(Revelation 17:3-6)*

At the moment it is supposition that Europa represents the coming kingdom of the Antichrist, but it is interesting that this image should be adopted by Europe, when it has no seeming relevance to its activities. However, on one thing we can be clear, the European Union is becoming increasingly hostile to Christianity and Christians, all under the humanist banner of equality and human rights.

5. The final point is to note the enormous battle within the United Kingdom to come out of Europe which continued for over four years after the people had voted to leave. Parliament gave the right to the people of Britain to decide whether they wanted to stay in the EU or come out. They voted by a majority of 52% to 48% to come out of Europe. Parliament enacted Article 50 of the EU Constitution initiating Britain's exit. The two main parties (Conservative and Labour) promised to honour the referendum vote in their election manifestos for the election in 2017, and yet it took several years for this to become a reality. It is impossible not to see the hand of our spiritual enemy resisting any attempt to leave. This has indeed been confirmed in prophecies given by respected present-day prophets[6]. There were many groups praying for Brexit, but regrettably the majority of the Church does not understand the spiritual significance of this battle.

Why was it essential for Britain to leave the European Union?

In 1947, shortly before his death a famous Christian evangelist with a powerful healing ministry, Smith Wigglesworth, gave the following prophecy about the Church in Britain:

> *During the next few decades there will be two distinct moves of the Holy Spirit across the Church in Great Britain. The first move will affect every church that is open to receive it and will be characterised by restoration of the baptism and gifts of the Holy Spirit.*
>
> *The second move of the Holy Spirit will result in people leaving historic churches and planting new churches.*
>
> *In the duration of each of these moves, the people who are involved will say 'This is a great revival.' But the Lord says 'No, neither is this the great revival but both are steps towards it.' When the new church phase is on the wane, there will be evidenced in the churches something that has not been seen before: a coming together of those with an emphasis on the Word and those with an emphasis on the Spirit.*
>
> *When the Word and the Spirit come together, there will be the biggest movement of the Holy Spirit that the nation, and indeed, the world has ever seen. It will mark the beginning of a revival that will eclipse anything that has been witnessed within these shores, even the Wesleyan and the Welsh revivals of former years. The outpouring of God's Spirit will flow over from the United Kingdom to the mainland of Europe, and from there, will begin a missionary move to the ends of the earth.*

Other Christian leaders have had a similar picture of revival fires starting in the United Kingdom. It does seem, despite the rejection of Christianity in this country and the apostasy of belief in many parts of the Church, that God does have a destiny for Britain to fulfil. I believe this destiny could not be achieved while we were still in spiritual bondage to the satanic principality in charge of the European Union. It was essential that we leave if we are to fulfil this destiny.

NOTES

1. The United Kingdom was taken into the European Economic Community (Common Market, EEC) by the Conservative government led by Prime Minister Edward Heath in 1973 without a referendum. Harold Wilson's Labour government then gave the British people a referendum in 1975 on whether they wished to remain in the EEC. That time the public voted overwhelmingly to remain in the EEC by a majority of 34% of the votes cast. What the public did not know at the time is that European leaders were already thinking of the economic, political and financial union which began to happen 20 years later (Maastricht Treaty 1993) with the formation of the European Union and which in the eye of today's leaders is still not complete

2. The Holy Roman Empire was an attempt to revive the Western Roman Empire which had collapsed in AD 476. It was a powerful aggregate of states under its first emperor Charlemagne covering France, Germany, Italy and other European States, but over time it gradually lost territory and influence.

3. The European Union has divided Europe into administrative areas under the heading **Interreg** (interregional cooperation). The ostensible purpose for this is to flag up **Transnational Co-operation**. Until recently we were in Interreg V (2014-2020) [Google: ERDF Transnational Co-operation plans]. These programmes are known as the **European Cohesion Policy**. The Lisbon Treaty (1995) refers to economic, social and **territorial** cohesion. Within these macro-regions of Europe the intention is to bring these areas into economic and social alignment for infrastructure, grants, projects and other activity and each region will have its own transnational assembly. Prior to leaving the European Union the United Kingdom would have been affected by three of these regions:

TransManche	Southern England and Northern France
Atlantic Area	The West coast of Scotland, all of Ireland, Wales and the West country and then on through Western France, Northern Spain and Portugal
North Sea/Baltic Area	Eastern Scotland and England down to Kent then North Sea coastal areas including Denmark around to southern Sweden.

   While at present these alignments do not affect the territorial integrity of individual states it is clear that much work has already been done. The EU is continuing to set up the regions of a future European super-state when national boundaries will disappear. This is a slow operation that is proceeding very much under the radar and with the seemingly admirable idea of co-operation between constituent parts of nations within the EU. There was considerable consternation in some of Britain's national papers about ten years ago when the Conservatives came to power and discovered what had been happening under the Labour Government in the period 1997 to 2010. Now however it all seems to have fallen out of the news.

(The maps for transnational cooperation can be found on the Internet by Googling: 'maps of interreg countries'. Those for the period 2014-2020 still display the parts of the United Kingdom that were involved in this period. For the later period 2021-2027 the United Kingdom has been removed, as we would expect.)

4. The reason we cannot be entirely sure that the EU Parliament building in Strasbourg represents the Tower of Babel is because the architects are said to have based their design on ancient Roman amphitheatres.

    The issue was further complicated by a poster known as the "Construction Site Poster" which did depict the Tower of Babel as painted by Brueghel with a modern crane and the caption: "Europe: many tongues, one voice". This poster was withdrawn under protest and was in fact produced by the Council of Europe, not the same organisation as the European Union. Nevertheless, the caption is likely to resonate with the views of the EU and it clearly reverses what God did at the time of Babel!

5. The Rape of Europa is a mythological Greek story. The chief god of the Greeks was Zeus who became infatuated with Europa, a beautiful young Phoenician girl. In order to get his way with her and to avoid the suspicion of his wife Hera, Zeus metamorphoses into a beautiful white bull. The girl is fascinated by this handsome creature, caresses him and climbs onto his back. Zeus (as the bull) then abducts the young woman to Crete where he reveals his true identity, rapes and impregnates her. Europa gives birth to a son Minos, who grows up to become the King of Crete. One has to ask why such a myth so fascinates the hierarchy of the EU – why should they want to make it an emblem on coins, and in artwork?

6. David Noakes has given several prophecies about the need for Britain to exit the European Union, while David Hathaway has long campaigned for us to come out. David Noake's prophecies can be found by 'Googling: *David Noakes - prophecy'*. The relevant prophecies are dated November 2015; 11th September 2016 and 17th June 2017.

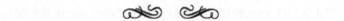

Appendix 6

How does the Church match up to a Victorious Army?

In Chapter 10 I listed nine aspects of a victorious military army. In this appendix I will briefly consider how the current Church, at least in the western world, matches up to such an army.

This appendix will inevitably highlight weaknesses in the universal Church's approach to the kingdom of darkness. I want to acknowledge therefore that there are many church leaders who do recognise the importance of waging war against Satan and his kingdom and are actually doing so. Furthermore, many also recognise how important it is to work together with other churches in prayer and in evangelism.

However, I believe that I am right in saying that most churches, for whatever reason, lack an understanding of Satan and his kingdom and of the need to tackle it.

A victorious army?

Having discussed the nature of the spiritual warfare against Satan, and the weapons available to the universal Church, we are in a position to compare the Church to a natural human army. How does it match up to a victorious military army? Let us examine each aspect in turn. A note of caution is in order: The Church can act like an army, but it is not a military organisation. Such differences will be highlighted and need to be borne in mind.

1. The Church most certainly has a **cause** which its soldiers can share and believe in. This cause is God's salvation for the human race.

2. The Church most certainly has a **leader** whom it can **trust**. This leader is, of course, the risen Jesus Christ who stands far above any human or military leader in history.

3. A **chain of command** which the soldiers understand. The universal Church does not have a hierarchy of leadership such as is found in a human army or indeed in some of the church denominations.

    The New Testament Church does, however, have a structure adequate for the task assigned to it by its Captain-General. It has leaders who are appointed with the help of the Holy Spirit to oversee the church in a particular locality. The pastor has associate leaders: apostle, prophet, teacher and evangelist (*Ephesians 4*) who have specific functions in the local church and its neighbourhood. The neighbourhood envisaged in the New Testament was a city or town. This was not intended to be served by **independent** local churches, such as we have in the modern world.

    In the early years of the Church, there was what could be considered a universal leadership. This was the Council at Jerusalem which settled matters of doctrine. Once the canon of scripture, the clearly defined written Word of God, had been settled by the end of the fourth century AD[1], there was much less need for such a universal leadership.

    Today, most churches are denominational and therefore have national (or even worldwide) leaderships. There is clearly a need for co-operation at this level when the church is praying over national and governmental issues (for example, Brexit or unrighteous laws). However, with the fixed denominational structures this is difficult to achieve, and this is why my suggested strategy concentrates much more on the local church.

A major difference from a human army

The Church is different from a national army in one very significant respect. Its Captain-General, Jesus Christ, working through his Holy Spirit, has access to and therefore knowledge about every part of his Body, the Church. He has established a role for the Church with structure and guidelines as to how it should operate, but it means that every individual church needs to consult its Captain-General for whatever new activity they undertake. Much day-to-day guidance is given in God's Word, the Bible, but new ventures, especially spiritual warfare, always need consultation with the Lord Jesus Christ.

There is a further difference from a human army. It is possible for every member of the universal church to receive instructions directly from Christ himself via the Holy Spirit. A human army seldom functions like this and for good reason – confusion of command. However, every church leader should be aware that Christ may choose to speak through the humblest member of the congregation. Unlike a natural army this is not a recipe for confusion. The need for order and submission to church leadership is clearly laid out in the apostle Paul's writings (for example, *1 Corinthians 11-12* and *14*). It does mean that every leader needs to remain humble and be on the lookout for the word of the Lord from an unexpected quarter.

4. As we have seen in Chapter 12 the Church is most definitely **equipped with armour and weaponry**, both defensive and offensive. This is fully up to date in the warfare with Satan.

5. An army that **knows and understands the enemy**. On this matter the Church is ill prepared. Many Christians have only the vaguest idea that they face a formidable and well-organised enemy. As mentioned earlier, many believers think or are taught that they should stay well clear of this subject: Satan may tempt them, and they should resist the temptation. Other than this he should be left well alone. Christian leaders may be equally unaware of Satan's influence upon the human race.

6. Soldiers who are **trained, fit** and **disciplined**. Once again, the Church is not prepared. If one is not properly aware of the enemy, then one is unlikely to be ready to tackle him. Much of the Church is simply unaware that they are meant to be soldiers in Christ's army. If they are aware, they are not necessarily trained or ready for the spiritual battle.

7. The Church is certainly **not united**. There are countless denominations and groupings with different theological views

and liturgical practices. The Church's long history, with decisive help from its enemy, Satan, has been responsible for this fragmentation and the apostasy found in many churches.

Over the last 500 years God has worked to reverse this apostasy. It started with the Reformation and the publication of the Bible in native languages that people could understand, rather than in Latin which only the priests could understand. Over the following centuries God began to restore New Testament Church government and practice. The nineteenth and twentieth centuries saw much restoration of biblical truth: faith in the Bible as the Word of God, full immersion baptism, the restoration of the gifts of the Holy Spirit in the Pentecostal and Charismatic movements. These movements themselves created new denominations each with some aspect of biblical truth.

My conclusion from this state of affairs is that God works with the Church as it stands at any stage in history. He does not want all these movements to coalesce into one large, united Church, based on New Testament practice. Such an upheaval, were anyone to attempt it, would have cataclysmic consequences for the Church at a time when many Christians believe we are in the days approaching Christ's return to earth.

What I do think, however, is that **God wants the existing churches and denominations to co-operate, to work together at both a local and national level**. They will retain their distinct features, but set aside theological and liturgical differences, and thus be able to work towards a united battle plan for their locality. I described how this might happen in Chapters 13 & 14.

8. The Church does not have **an effective battle plan** either nationally or locally. Given the observations under points 5 and 7, it is hardly likely that they would have such a plan. At the local level, most individual churches follow their own agenda and organise their own evangelistic outreaches. Sometimes local churches will co-operate for a citywide day of prayer or for a visiting evangelist, but it rarely leads to sustained co-operative activity.

It is at the local level: city, town or countryside, **where the co-operation really matters**. Once such co-operation and unity become established practice in taking the battle to the enemy, then we shall see a shift in the spiritual realm. The enemy will be on the back foot, the spiritual atmosphere will change, and many more people will find salvation and join God's kingdom.

9. The last point: the universal Church and its local manifestations are certainly not **adept at either defence or offence**. Churches have probably thought more about defence than offence because they meet Satan's attacks in their congregations. Many churches have good pastoral facilities aimed at taking care of new converts and ministering to the flock. This approach, however, is inward looking. A church might find some of its pastoral problems diminishing if it took the offensive against Satan's activities in the church and local neighbourhood.

Conclusion

Assessing how the universal and the local church matches up to the characteristics of a victorious military army makes an interesting study. Where the characteristics (points 1 to 4) depend mostly on God's provision, the Church has a template for victory. Where the characteristics (points 5 to 9) are largely down to leaders and ordinary believers, the church is far from victorious.

We cannot lay all responsibility at God's door. We have already seen that in setting up the Church God has created a partnership with believers in which he asks them to participate in what he is doing on earth. He does his part, if we are prepared to do ours. I think it is a brilliant strategy because he asks converts to Christ to participate in bringing other people to the faith. Once rescued from Satan's kingdom, they can help to rescue others.

Jesus described humanity as a harvest field in which the Church gets to harvest people for the kingdom. Because humanity has an enemy in the person of Satan, we have to understand this enemy and his tactics and then to overcome him through spiritual warfare.

Chapter 13 attempted to demonstrate how the Church might begin to overcome these weaknesses.

NOTES

1. The Canon of scripture is that collection of biblical books which constitute the acknowledged written Word of God. For the Protestant churches this means the 39 books of the Old Testament plus the 27 books of the New Testament (66 in all). Other historical denominations like the Catholic and Orthodox churches may include further books belonging to what is often called the Apocrypha.

    Many Christians do not realise that the New Testament Canon took several centuries before it was finally agreed. (The Old Testament scriptures were agreed by the Jews as their Tanach by the end of the first century AD). This was partly because believers were at first able to rely on witness accounts of the events described in the New Testament. It is surprising to find that some of the books we so prize today such as Hebrews were not at first considered to be authentic scripture.

    The Canon is important because we can rely on the Holy Spirit to illuminate the scriptures to us. This does not mean that other books are not valuable. I and II Maccabees, for example, provide valuable history, but I believe the scriptures need to belong to the Canon **for God to breathe spiritual life into them**.

    My own view is that God was happy to allow the Canon to take time to bed down, but that what we have now is his final written Word which cannot be added to or subtracted from.

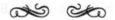

Bibliography

Baker, H.A, *Visions beyond the Veil* (UK: Sovereign World 2000)

Cross, David, *God's Covering – A Place of Healing* (UK: Sovereign World 2008)

Dawson, John, *Taking our Cities for God* (Florida: Charisma House 2001)

Dunman, Mark, *Has God really finished with Israel?* (UK: Freedom Publishing 2nd edition 2022)
Dunman, Mark, *The Return of Jesus Christ* (London: New Wine Press 2015)

Frangipane, Francis, *The Three Battlegrounds* (British Edition: New Wine Press 1994)*
Frangipane, Francis, *The House of the Lord* (Florida: Creation House 1991)

Hathaway, David, *Why Siberia?* (UK: Eurovision Publications 1995)

Grubb, Norman, *Rees Howells Intercessor* (Cambridge: The Lutterworth Press 1952/2005)*

Horrobin, Peter, *Healing through Deliverance* (Vol. 1 & 2, Foundation & Practice)* (UK: Sovereign World, 2003)

Hughes, Pat & Hyde, Gay, *Helps to Intercession and Spiritual Warfare* (Private Publication)*

LeClaire, Jennifer, Waging Prophetic Warfare (Florida, Charisma House 2016)*

MacArthur, John, *Our Awesome God* (Illinois: Crossway Books 2001)

MacNutt, Francis, *The Healing Reawakening* (Michigan: Chosen Books 2006)*

Maton, Richard, *Samuel Rees Howells – a Life of Intercession* (By Faith Media 2018)

Prince, Derek, *War in Heaven* (UK: Derek Prince Ministries-UK 2003)

Rallo, Vito, *Breaking Generational Curses & Pulling Down Strongholds* (Florida: Creation House 2000)

Stevens, Selwyn, *Unmasking Freemasonry (Removing the Hoodwink)* *

Ten Boom, Corrie, *The Hiding Place* (UK: Hodder & Stoughton 2004)

Tidy, David, *Discerning The Mixture – Spiritual/Natural* (UK: Prayer Warriors International)*

Waring, Emma, *Seasons of Sex and Intimacy* (UK: Hullo Creative Ltd 2018)

* Books that readers may find helpful concerning spiritual warfare and individual ministry.

GLOSSARY

Allegory is an extended metaphor. There is a sense of an unfolding story. For example, Jesus Christ is described as the Lion of the Tribe of Judah (*Revelation 5:5*). This is a simple metaphor. On the other hand the Valley of Dry Bones in *Ezekiel Chapter 37* is an allegory for the restoration of the nation of Israel. The story unfolds as the bones come to life and we are told that they represent the whole house of Israel.

Anti-Semitism is belief or behaviour which is hostile to Jews simply because they are Jewish.

Apologetics is the intellectual defence of Christianity.

Apocalypse (lit. *unveiling*) is the prophetic revelation given to the Apostle John as recorded in the book of *Revelation*. **Apocalyptic** means pertaining to this revelation; prophesying disaster or doom.

Apostasy means falling away from the Christian faith. It can also be used in relation to other faiths and political causes.

Apostle: The twelve apostles of Jesus Christ were the human founders of the Christian Church, (led of course by the Holy Spirit). An apostle is someone with a call to spread the gospel by planting or founding churches.

Apostolic Church, sometimes called the New Testament Church, is significant in that it is thought to provide a template for the way churches, in any age, should function.

Ark of the Covenant. This was the wooden vessel inlaid with gold and with carved Cherubim with outstretched wings where God's presence chose to dwell on earth for the Israelites. It was first constructed for the Tabernacle in the wilderness as Israel journeyed to the Promised Land and then transferred to the Temple built by King Solomon in Jerusalem. Only the High Priest, and that once a year, was allowed to enter the chamber (the Most Holy Place) which housed the Ark, for the purpose of atoning for the sins of Israel.

Ba'al, Molech and Ashtoreth are three of the principal **pagan** gods of Cana'an. They were associated with abominable religious practices such as sacrifice of children in the fire to the god Molech. Israel was strictly forbidden to associate with the Cana'anite peoples and their practices, but were frequently seduced into adopting such practices. These 'gods' of course were nothing less than a cover for Satan's pagan activities.

Born-Again means the renewal of one's spirit by coming into a personal relationship with Jesus Christ. It comes from Jesus' words to Nicodemus in *John Chapter 3*.

Canon of Scripture is the list of books considered to be inspired by the Holy Spirit and which therefore constitute the Bible as we know it today. The process of consolidating the canon was spread over time. The Old Testament canon (which the Jews call the *Tanach*) was thought to have been completed by the end of the first century AD, possibly at a Council of Jamnia circa AD 90. The New Testament canon (of 27 books), however, was not settled until the end of the fourth century AD, where it was accepted as closed at the Council of Carthage in AD 397 under the leadership of St. Augustine.

Charismatic Revival refers to the Holy Spirit Renewal in the traditional churches from the middle of the twentieth century. This led to Christians being 'baptised in the Holy Spirit' with the accompaniment of supernatural gifts such as prophecy and 'speaking in tongues'. It had been preceded by the Pentecostal awakening earlier in the century with the establishment of Pentecostal denominations.

Church Fathers were the leading Christian theologians in the early centuries of the Church, ending with St. Augustine in the fourth century AD. They were especially significant in Church history as they formulated doctrine in the years before the *Canon of Scripture* was finalised.

Covenant is a binding, unbreakable obligation between two parties which in former times was sealed in blood. It is a solemn undertaking between two people or groups of people; or between God and a person or group of persons. The most significant covenants are those which express God's relationship with people.

Crusaders were soldiers mainly from France and Northern Europe in the early Middle Ages (circa 1095-1291) who led a series of campaigns (Crusades) to win back Jerusalem and the Holy Land for Christianity from Muslim control. They were anything but Christian in action, slaughtering Muslims, Jews and even local Christians, in their attempts.

Dispensationalism is the theology which divides biblical history into distinct periods or ages, (most commonly seven). Each dispensation represents a different way in which God works with mankind in salvation history. The last two: 'the Church age' and 'the Kingdom (Millennial) age' are the two relevant ages to a contemporary view of Israel. Dispensationalists tend to think the Church age has run its course and that God has now turned his attention back to Israel. (Some writers - this author included - would argue that the theology of the Church and Israel does not have to be an 'either the Church or Israel' theology. It can be both.)

Dominionism This is a modern version of the Postmillennial view of Christ's Second Coming to earth. It argues that as more souls are won for Christ the world will become a better place, governments will become more Christian and eventually the world will be made ready for Christ's return. It stands in stark contrast to the Premillennial view which argues that in the last days the world will become much darker spiritually and Christ will come back to defeat the Antichrist and forces of darkness and then usher in the millennial age.

Ecclesiology is the theological study of the Christian Church: its origin, its relationship to Jesus Christ, its relationship to believers, its role in salvation and its destiny.

Eschatology is the doctrine of the end-times, both preceding and following Christ's return to earth.

Evangelical Christian is one who has had a personal encounter with the risen Jesus Christ and who feels motivated to share the Good News.

Exegesis is the explanation or interpretation of scripture.

Gospel: This is the good news of forgiveness of sins and salvation through Jesus Christ. It refers also to one of the four accounts of the life of Jesus in the New Testament.

Great Tribulation (Jacob's Trouble): This is the time of very great trouble coming upon the world in the period prior to the Second Advent or the return of Jesus Christ, and which will be centred on the land of Israel and the Middle East. There are many prophecies in the Old Testament and passages in the New Testament which refer to such a time. Some writers believe, from passages in *Daniel* and *Revelation*, that the duration of this time of trouble will be seven years. Other writers think this time has already happened with the destruction of the Temple in AD 70, but this view is difficult to sustain in the face of passages from the New Testament, especially *Matthew Chapter 24* and the book of *Revelation*. (See the author's book: *The Return of Jesus Christ.*)

Heaven. Heaven has several meanings. The first is the sky or atmosphere above our heads, the natural heaven. The second or mid-heaven (heavenly places) is the invisible domain of Satan and his fallen angels, while the third heaven (also invisible to the natural eye) is where God dwells along with his angels and saved humanity and from where he rules and reigns over the earth and the universe.

Hermeneutics denotes the art and science of text interpretation. In biblical hermeneutics, the *allegorical*, *typological* and *literal* would be different ways of understanding scripture.

Idolatry is the worship of a false god. This god may be represented by an **idol** such as an inanimate carving in wood or stone, or it may be an idea or a person.

Intercessory Prayer: Literally this means prayer on behalf of a person or situation, as distinct from adoratory, confessional or thanksgiving prayers. However, with the advent of the *charismatic* movement it has come to mean prayers motivated and led by the Holy Spirit himself – prayers which really engage God with the person or situation being prayed for.

Islam (Islamic or Muslim faith): Islam is the monotheistic religion founded by Muhammad in the seventh century AD and which spread rapidly across the Middle East. Its adherents are known as Muslims. Today it holds sway in all Arab countries and many others. Its holy book is the Qu'ran and its god is called Allah. It has two main sects, the majority Sunnis and the minority Shia, and its religious and social law is known as Sharia (Islamic Law). Militant Muslims desire all Islamic countries (and eventually the rest of the world) to be governed by Sharia Law. Islam is in opposition to the Christian faith. It denies that Jesus Christ is the Son of God and that salvation is found through his atoning death on the Cross.

Israelite: The term given to a citizen of Israel from the time of the *Exodus* until the division of Solomon's kingdom. Thereafter citizens tended to be called Jews, especially after the partial return from Babylon. Israelite is occasionally used in the New Testament.

Jew: The term Jew came to replace the word Israelite at the time of the Babylonian captivity. It is derived from Judah, the fourth son of Jacob. It probably came into widespread use because it was principally the people of Judah who returned from Babylon to rebuild the Temple and later on, the walls of Jerusalem.

Justification by faith: This means that we have been made righteous in God's sight. Because of the sacrifice of Jesus and the punishment which he took for our sin, God has cancelled our sin and we are seen as righteous in his sight. This is the free gift of God received through his unmerited favour or grace. We have done (and can do) nothing to merit this favour.

Kingdom of God: This kingdom is the rule of God in the hearts of all created beings who are willingly subject to him and thus in fellowship with him. This excludes unregenerate man, the devil and his fallen angels who, as the Bible makes very clear, are in rebellion against God.

Literalism: This refers to the *hermeneutic* whereby prophetic scripture is understood to have a literal, rather than an allegorical meaning.

Millennium: A period of 1000 years when Christ reigns on earth during a time of peace and blessing. It is mentioned specifically in *Revelation 20:5*, but it is thought that several passages in Isaiah are describing such a period e.g. *Isaiah 11:6-9, 65:20-25*. Christians may believe that this is a literal period in history or that it is symbolic, and this has led to sharply different views. (See the author's book: *The Return of Jesus Christ*.)

Messianic Jew: These are Jews who have come to a personal faith in Jesus Christ as their saviour and messiah. They are in God's family along with Gentile Christians, but prefer to be known as Messianic believers as a means of retaining their identity as Jews.

Metaphor is a figure of speech in which one object (or being) is described as another object (or being) in order to illustrate or emphasise its nature. For example, Jesus describes himself as the vine and believers as its branches.

Mosaic Law: This was the set of laws and commands given by God to the Israelites through Moses for governing every aspect of their lives. It was headed by the Moral Law or Ten Commandments and consisted in total of 613 statutes (mitzvot) including the two Genesis commands, "be fruitful and multiply" and male circumcision.

New Covenant: The New Covenant was first announced for the Jews in *Jeremiah 31:31-34*. It was enacted when Jesus died on the Cross for the sins of mankind and was then resurrected. For those who accept this sacrifice on their behalf, both Jew and Gentile, God gives them a new heart and writes his law upon it. It both fulfils and takes the place of the Old (Mosaic) Covenant.

New Heavens and Earth: This concerns the promise of God that the existing heavens and earth will be burnt up and new ones created in their place. It is referred to in both the Old Testament (*Isaiah 65:17* and *66:22*) and the New Testament (*2 Peter 3:7* and *Revelation 21:1*).

Occult Beliefs (lit. *hidden*): These are beliefs and practices pertaining to Satan's kingdom of darkness. Readers of the Bible are explicitly warned (*Deuteronomy 18:10-12*) against involvement in any kind of witchcraft, divination, fortune telling or contact with the dead.

Old Earth Creationism

(See *Young earth creationism* below).

Old Covenant: This is the covenant inaugurated between God and Moses who represented the Israelites. It is often called the *Mosaic Law* and is not to be confused with the Abrahamic Covenant. It set down the rules by which the Israelites should govern their relationship with God and between themselves, as the people were about to enter statehood as a nation.

Paganism: The word pagan relates to religion derived from nature and the material world. Paganism rejects monotheistic religion. It tends to believe in a plurality of gods (polytheism) and to ascribe a living soul to inanimate objects (animism). It ranges from celebrating nature to full involvement with the Occult. **Pagan practices** in the Old Testament were often morally repugnant, and abhorrent to God.

Parable is an allegorical narrative of real or imagined events from which a moral is drawn for the listener. The Parable was a popular teaching method with Jesus.

Para-church Organisations are bodies of Christian leaders that function outside the structure of a national or local church. They have grown up to meet particular needs that church members find are not being met within their own churches. They also have expertise in matters such as healing, and deliverance that may be beyond the capabilities of a small local church. Many church leaders welcome this expertise and recognise that God has appointed these ministries. Larger churches may feel that all Christian activity should take place under the authority of their own local or national church. A well directed Para-church organisation usually seeks the approval of the church before it agrees to minister to a church member.

Pentecost (Feast of Weeks, Hebrew *Shavuot*): The Day of Pentecost was the occasion described in *Acts Chapter 2* when the Holy Spirit fell on the assembled disciples of Jesus and they were supernaturally empowered to "speak in tongues" and to preach the gospel. In modern times **Pentecostal** has come to mean the reappearance of the experience of the Baptism in the Holy Spirit in the Christian Church, such as happened in the *Acts of the Apostles*. Churches espousing this experience are called Pentecostal.

Prophecy in the Bible is a supernatural revelation from God. It may reveal his heart for his people or his views on a subject, or it may be a message revealing future events. In the time of the Old Testament, speaking through **Prophets** was God's way of warning Israel, and urging them to return to him and his laws.

Protestant Church: This was the Church which emerged from the break with the Catholic Church during the Reformation in the sixteenth century. The Reformation, spearheaded by Martin Luther, affirmed the principles of **justification by faith alone** (i.e. not by good works), **the priesthood of all believers** and **the authority of the Bible** as God's revealed word to humanity. The Reformation encouraged people to read the Bible for themselves. It did away with the mediatory role of the priests and the idolatry of Mary, the mother of Jesus. It encouraged believers to relate directly to God in prayer, within the context of Church authority. There are today many denominations within the Protestant Church who vary in aspects of theology or Church practice, but all subscribe to this overarching theology.

Rapture: The Rapture is a phenomenon whereby one particular generation of Christians will not die, but be translated directly to heaven either shortly before or at the time of the Second Advent of Jesus Christ. Christians dispute the reality of the Rapture depending upon their millennial view of Christ's return (see **Millennium**), but two scriptures do seem to testify to such an event (*1 Thessalonians 4:13-18* and *1 Corinthians 15:50-52*). (See the author's book: *The Return of Jesus Christ.*)

Reformation, (see **Protestant Church**).

Replacement Theology holds that the promises concerning Israel in the Old Testament find their fulfilment in Christ and/or the Church in the New Testament. It is an alternative term for *Supersessionism* and *Fulfilment Theology*.

Revival is a spiritual awakening of the Church to the things of God leading to large numbers of non-Christians coming to faith in Christ through personal evangelism and evangelistic crusades. A true revival is always undergirded by a move of the Holy Spirit himself. Church history has seen many such revivals.

Rule of Double Reference is one of the rules that has been discerned for understanding the Bible. A passage of scripture may be speaking of two persons or events which are separated by a long interval of time, but which seem to be fused into one picture. This rule is particularly important for a correct understanding of prophecy. We saw this in the text in *Isaiah 14:12-14* where the writer is referring to the King of Babylon, but also to an angelic being whom we understand to be Lucifer/Satan.

Salvation is the process whereby we recognise that we are sinners in the sight of a holy God, and accept his solution through the death of Jesus Christ on the Cross. When we do this we are forgiven our sin, and our spirit is regenerated by the Holy Spirit. We are saved from judgement by God and said to be 'born-again' to spend eternity with him.

Sanctification is the process whereby the Holy Spirit works in our life to make us holy, that means separated to God and separated from the sinful world. Whereas *justification* is an instant event following *salvation* in which we are seen as righteous by God, sanctification is a process taking place over time. (It is only fair to say that some Christian teachers see sanctification as a state of holiness, rather than a process of becoming holy).

Second Advent (of Jesus Christ): This refers to the return of Christ at the end of the age. It is prophesied in both the Old and New Testaments. Few evangelical Christians doubt that this will be a literal return of the Lord Jesus Christ as a reigning King, though there are numerous variations in belief as to when and how this will happen. (See the author's book: *The Return of Jesus Christ.*)

Simile: A comparison of one thing with another to emphasise a particular aspect in the first. For example, a man might be described as being "as strong as a lion". A simile does not go as far as a *metaphor* in making the comparison.

Sorcery is witchcraft or deep participation in the Occult.

Tabernacle: The Tabernacle was the tent of meeting between God and his people. Moses was given instructions about how to build this on Mount Sinai, while the Israelites were still en route to the Promised Land. The system of Priests and Levites (assistant priests) together with the extensive system of animal sacrifice were all instituted for the Tabernacle. The presence of God dwelt in the inner sanctum, the Most Holy Place. The Tabernacle was later replaced by a permanent building, the *Temple*.

Talmud: The Talmud is the collective writings of rabbis over the centuries on numerous topics including law, ethics, philosophy, customs, history, and practical subjects like medicine, agriculture and hygiene. It is known as The Oral Law in contrast to the *Torah* which is the written Law of Moses. For centuries it was conveyed orally, but following the destruction of the Second Temple (AD 70) it came to be written down in the early centuries AD. It is over 6000 pages long and contains the views of countless rabbis. It quotes the Hebrew Bible (*Tanach*) at least once on every page. It is used as a guide to interpreting the *Torah*.

Tanach: The Tanach is the Hebrew Bible; that which the Church calls *The Old Testament*.

Temple: The Temple was central to Jewish belief and practice in the Old Testament. It took the place of the Tabernacle, first built while the Israelites were still on the move. King David desired to build a permanent home as a dwelling place for the Lord's presence, but this privilege was granted to his son, Solomon, who built the magnificent **First Temple**. This embodied the system of Priests and Levites and all the practices which belonged to the Tabernacle. This Temple was destroyed by Nebuchadnezzar when the people of Judah went into exile in Babylon. It was rebuilt as the **Second Temple** under the leadership of Zerubbabel when the Jews were allowed to return after seventy years of exile. (This Temple was completed circa 516 BC.) Although built to replicate the First Temple, it lacked certain items such as the **Ark of the Covenant** and the Tablets of Stone which had been lost at the time of the First Temple's destruction. According to Jewish tradition, it also lacked the Shekinah glory or Presence of God. This Temple was then enlarged and made more magnificent by Herod the Great in the first century BC. The Second Temple was the one destroyed by the Romans in AD 70.

Theocracy is government directly from God, mediated by priests. This was the government instituted by God for the Israelites through Moses. God was disappointed and offended when the Israelites sought a king to rule over them during the time of Samuel, but they were still bound by the Mosaic Law.

Theology is the in-depth study of the Jewish and Christian faiths. It deals with God's nature, his attributes and his relationship to his creation. It uses the Bible as its primary source.

Torah: The Torah is the Pentateuch or first five books of the Old Testament. It contains the Jewish written law as distinct from the *Talmud* or oral law which is used by rabbis to interpret the written law.

Trinity or Tri-une God. This is the existence of the one true God in three distinct Persons, the Father, the Son (Jesus Christ) and the Holy Spirit. They work as a unity in complete harmony which is why the passage in *Deuteronomy 6:4* is able to say: "Hear Oh Israel: the Lord our God , the Lord is one."

Typology is a *hermeneutic* in which Old Testament 'types' are seen as being fulfilled in the New Testament. For example, Joseph is seen as a 'type' to represent Jesus, while the prospective sacrifice of Isaac by his father Abraham is seen as a 'type' for the crucifixion of God's Son. It does not exclude a *literalist* hermeneutic running parallel to a typological one.

Young Earth Creationism is the view that the universe and earth and all life upon the earth was formed in the six days of creation described in Genesis. This contrasts with **Old Earth Creationism** which believes that God created all life (it did not evolve), but that the days of Genesis may have been longer intervals of time and not 24 hour days. An alternative view is that the days were 24 hour days, but that this was a new creation of life on an old earth in which previous life had been destroyed by a world wide flood. Proponents of this view say that this would explain the existence of the dinosaurs which many people find difficult to accommodate in the young earth scenario.

INDEXES

INDEX OF SCRIPTURE REFERENCES

See also useful scriptures under Appendix 4

GENERAL INDEX

The appendices are not included in this general index. The words God, Christ & Satan are used so frequently in the text that only a few are highlighted in this index.

Y

Z